SUPERNATURAL UPGRADE

DESTINY IMAGE BOOKS BY
CHAZDON STRICKLAND

Racism, the Church, and the Nation

SUPERNATURAL UPGRADE

KEYS TO WALKING IN THE
GLORY REALM

CHAZDON STRICKLAND

DESTINY IMAGE® PUBLISHERS, INC.
P.O. Box 310, Shippensburg, PA 17257-0310
"Promoting Inspired Lives."

This book and all other Destiny Image and Destiny Image Fiction books are available at Christian bookstores and distributors worldwide.

For more information on foreign distributors, call 717-532-3040.
Reach us on the Internet: www.destinyimage.com.

ISBN 13 TP: 978-0-7684-6230-2
ISBN 13 eBook: 978-0-7684-6231-9

For Worldwide Distribution, Printed in the U.S.A.
1 2 3 4 5 6 7 8 / 26 25 24 23 22

DEDICATION

I dedicate this book to my beautiful wife, Emily, who has helped make every God-given dream come true. Without your love and encouragement, not only would this book not be possible, but the very ministry that God has called us to would not exist. I would not be the man I am today without you. You are the epitome of what it means to be a supportive and loving wife and mother. There is nothing better than having you with me on this journey. I have learned much from you and your relationship with Jesus. I call you "Jesus' best friend" and am always captivated and filled with childlike faith when you share with me the encounters you have with God. I love you, beautiful Emily.

I also dedicate this book to people who are hungry for God, but feel frustrated and misunderstood. You are not alone. People worldwide have the same hunger that is burning in you. You may feel this way because our generation is stepping through the door of revival. Keep seeking God. Pursue Him faithfully and you will see revival.

ACKNOWLEDGMENTS

I first acknowledge Jesus Christ. Without Him I would be nothing.

My wife and kids. Thank you for everything. Your love has propelled me to the highest heights. You have been with me through it all, and I love you all dearly.

My mom, my dad, my sister, and the rest of my family. Thank you for being just that, family. I love y'all.

My church, Ignite The Globe. I love you all. Thank you for allowing me to lead you.

Apostle Jennifer LeClaire. Thank you for being my covering and for writing the foreword to this book.

Larry Sparks and the Destiny Image crew. Thank you for the opportunity to write this book. I appreciate all of your hard work and behind-the-scenes fixing.

CONTENTS

FOREWORD

When I look at the Body of Christ today, I see a people who are tired of lifeless religion. I see a remnant who wants to demonstrate that Jesus is alive. I see believers who want a supernatural upgrade. After all, Jesus said we would do the greater works (see John 14:12). He's called us to cast out devils, heal the sick, cleanse the lepers, and even raise the dead (see Matthew 10:8).

Beyond the church world, a generation is rising that is curious about the supernatural realm and dissatisfied with the church as it has been handed down to them. They are burned out on religion, even though many have never stepped inside a church. As a result, they are seeking the supernatural outside of Christ. They are awed by what they don't realize are lying signs and wonders (2 Thessalonians 2:9). They are moving further than ever from the true God of the Supernatural.

What the church—and the world—needs is a spiritual awakening. A certain passage in Luke's gospel continues to strike my heart. Jesus took Peter, John and James up to a mountain to pray. As Jesus prayed, His face changed, and his clothes started radiating white light. Moses and Elijah appeared in the glory to discuss His assignment of salvation through the cross.

Unfortunately, during this epic event Peter, John and James fell asleep. Can you imagine? This is a picture of many in the church today.

God wants to bring us into supernatural glory encounters where we see people delivered, bodies healed, marriages restored— all in the blink of an eye. Too many of us have become familiar with worship, familiar with prophecy, and even familiar with the Holy Spirit. We go through the motions, half asleep. A spirit of slumber is working to squeeze out our supernatural upgrade.

But look what happens next. Luke 9:32 tells us, *"When they were fully awake, they saw His glory and the two men who stood with Him."* Catch that. They were not half awake. They were not mostly awake. They were fully awake. And they stayed awake. That experience on the Mount of Transfiguration marked them. Even though they would stagger over Christ's death on the cross, His resurrection rekindled the supernatural flame in their heart and they walked in signs, wonders, and miracles that we rarely see in today's church.

It's time to get back to our roots. It's time to wake up and receive our supernatural upgrade. Chazdon Strickland has written a guide for the hungry heart, for those believers who know there's more than what they've seen and don't merely want to witness it—but walk in it. Chazdon is uniquely qualified to lead the way, as he walks in the glory realm. I've ministered alongside him as he has ministered the Holy Spirit's power that drives out demons and results in extraordinary miracles.

Supernatural Upgrade demystifies the realms of the spirit, offering a blend of theology, activation prayers, inspiring stories, and practical instruction for walking in your supernatural upgrade. Reading the pages of this book, you'll discover there's no formula but there are patterns. There is no shortcut, but there is something called risky faith that will accelerate your journey into places your eye hasn't seen and your ear hasn't heard.

I believe you'll receive an impartation just from reading this book! It's packed with wisdom and revelation beyond Chazdon's years. He didn't learn what he knows from any man or any woman, but from following instructions from the Spirit of God and seeing undeniable, irreputable breakthroughs in the lives of those he ministers too—and even in his own family.

I wish we could get this book into the hands of every believer of every age. It will challenge you and encourage you at the same time. *Supernatural Upgrade* is like a field guide for new breed Christians who long to walk in spiritual realms; who long to see a book of Acts church again. Thank you, Chazdon, for penning this important contribution to the Body of Christ.

JENNIFER LECLAIRE
Author of *The Seer Dimensions*
Senior Leader, Awakening House of
Prayer Global Movement

INTRODUCTION

The Spirit of God is awakening the church! What if you could be used by God like Elijah, Peter, or Paul? A passion is rising in the hearts of all of God's people for a move of God in our generation. A desire to see Jesus has been kindled and is burning in the hearts of Christians all around the world. Like in the early church, the Holy Spirit—the breath of God—is awakening the hearts of people and aligning the church with its true purpose, which is to express Christ's glory on earth through His children, the believers.

The fire of revival is increasing and will climax with a global revival that will revive the church, awaken the world, and lead to an unprecedented harvest of souls. God is releasing revelation knowledge worldwide to accelerate His church into glory. His unprecedented manifested glory will cover the earth. The world will be *"turned upside down"* (Acts 17:6 NKJV) by the modern church as the Kingdom of God is demonstrated in an undeniable way. It will be a full-scale invasion of the glory of God on earth through God's people! The church will be supernaturally upgraded!

This book is for everyone who is hungry and thirsty to be used in the end-time move of God in power and demonstration. It is good to know our biblical history—and the past should encourage us to experience God for ourselves *now* and in the future. We can no longer settle to just read about God moving or listen to stories about how God moved through His generals in the past. We must become hungry for the supernatural works of God to be revived *now.*

It's time for the church of our generation to come out of religious, powerless Christianity and walk with God in the supernatural. In this book, you will learn how to walk in God's powerful anointing and experience His glory through biblical and personal experiences. Let's start with the Bible's perspective.

God's People and His Glory

Exodus chapters 33 and 34 reveal what distinguishes God's people and what comprises God's glory. Believers are His children and partners in His glory when we ask Him to go alongside us as we journey through the glorious life He designed especially for each of us.

For example, when God tells Moses to take the Israelites to the Promised Land, Moses expresses a most important concern, *"If your Presence* [glory] *does not go with us, do not send us up from here. How will anyone know that you are pleased with me and with your people unless you go with us?"* And then Moses asks this rhetorical question, *"What will distinguish me and your people from all the other people on the face of the earth?"* (Exodus 33:15-17 NIV).

Moses wasn't demanding an answer. The question was the answer—what makes us different from other people is that our God goes with us; He walks with us. From creation, the very beginning, God's desire was and always has been to walk with us. The entirety of the Bible is an account of God drawing His people close to Him, to His light (see 1 John 1:7) and glory.

Isaiah 60:19 (NIV) tells us, *"The sun will no more be your light by day, nor will the brightness of the moon shine on you, for* the **Lord will be your everlasting light,** *and your* **God will be your glory.**" And *"Jesus said, 'Did I not tell you that **if you believe, you will see the glory of God?**'"* (John 11:40 NIV).

Moses heard the Lord reply, *"My Presence will go with you, and I will give you rest"* (Exodus 33:14 NIV). After the Lord told Moses that He would be with him and the people, "Then Moses said to the Lord, *"Now show me your glory."* The Lord's response is earthshaking:

And the Lord said, "I will cause all my goodness to pass in front of you, and I will proclaim my name, the Lord, in your presence..." (Exodus 33:19-23 NIV).

Later in the same conversation, the Lord and His servant, Moses, have the ultimate exchange:

Moses immediately threw himself to the ground and worshiped. And he said, "O Lord, if it is true that I have found favor with you, then please travel with us. Yes, this is a stubborn and rebellious people, but please forgive our iniquity and our sins. Claim us as your own special possession."

The Lord replied, "Listen, I am making a covenant with you in the presence of all your people. I will perform miracles that have never been performed anywhere in all the earth or in any nation. And all the people around you will see the power of the Lord—the awesome power I will display for you" (Exodus 34:8-10 NLT).

God wants to be present with you. He wants you to experience His glory and His power. He will perform miracles with you and through you. And you will be part of His supernatural, glorious upgrade.

1

THE SCHOOL
OF THE SPIRIT

*Jesus said, "I tell you the truth, anyone who
believes in me will do the same works I have
done, and even greater works, because I am going
to be with the Father"* (John 14:12 NLT).

Utter shock is the only way to describe the story I'm about
to tell you! What took place filled all of us with the awe and
wonder of Heaven!

I was in Riviera Beach, Florida, preaching at a conference themed "Fresh Oil." I remember standing on the stage and sharing about God's anointing. At first nothing significant was happening; I could feel the power of God building in the atmosphere, but nothing notable.

Then I moved out into a time of ministry and people began to fall under the power of the Holy Spirit, a normal occurrence in our ministry. Healings took place in people throughout the room— but I still knew there was more to experience. I am always thankful for all of the works of God being done, but His *greater works* impact people and glorify God in a way that nothing else can (see John 14:12).

And Then...

Because the conference was taking place during the covid pandemic, people were wearing masks. A young man approached me as I was praying, and I stopped and asked him what he needed from God. The young man did not respond, so I asked again. Still no response. I was getting ready to move on when his mother approached me and said her son had trouble verbalizing words because it was determined that 30 percent of his brain had permanent loss of function—that portion was dead. The doctors had pretty much declared him a vegetable and prescribed medicine that would make it easier as he died. It was horrible to hear her son's story. Medical science had declared its limits.

I'm thankful for medical science, but our God is supernatural and He has given us access to Himself, the living God, the Great Physician. I felt faith rise up in me and I laid my hands on the young man and prayed with divine boldness in Jesus' name. After I prayed, I took a step back and I saw a spirit leave him. Then the young man pulled his mask down and shouted, "My name is Travis!" At this point I didn't realize how miraculous his statement was.

I looked over at his mother and she exclaimed, "He couldn't talk like that!" She was amazed. Then the atmosphere was lifted into another dimension of the glory of God, and I realized that God wasn't finished with Travis yet. In the next instant, the young man took off running around the room full of energy and joy.

The glory of God increased and praise and worship erupted! The gathering reached a realm where there was no need for me to say anything more. God continued to move strongly for another hour or so after that miracle.

All Glory to God

This moment may make me seem to be a unicorn or some type of superhero, but actually there had been a time when I believed God would not use me in the supernatural. I knew many people who were uniquely gifted, but I was just so ordinary in my own eyes.

I attended a school of prophecy that lasted seven weeks. The school was remarkable and I was learning so much—things I had never heard before were teaching me the more of God. I was a babe in Christ at the time; consequently, it was a humbling time for me at the school. Each week I witnessed revelation gifts flowing, and each one manifested in a unique way through each person.

On the final day of the school, each student was required to prophesy. I watched in absolute amazement as each person was being encouraged. I could see people being deeply touched by God. I was the last student in the group to prophesy. I looked into the eyes of a woman over whom I was supposed to prophesy, but nothing came for me to say. I waited; I spoke in tongues; I did everything I was instructed to do, but still nothing prophetic came from my voice.

At this point, you are probably waiting for me to begin some epic comeback story; but unfortunately, for years this incident destroyed any confidence that I could hear from or even be used by God.

GOD USED MY DIFFICULTY TO LEAD ME TO PRAYER AND A CLOSER WALK WITH HIM.

As I stood there in front of the group of students and the prophet who was holding the training, the prophet began to say harsh things to me over the microphone. I was so embarrassed. I was flooded with thoughts of being a failure, and eventually I gave up. I concluded that night that the supernatural was real, but I wouldn't personally be part of it.

As difficult as that moment was for me, God used it for my benefit. Though it was an extremely humbling experience, it provoked me for more. I knew there was more of what God had for me, and I was hungry. I don't believe God planned my embarrassment, but He used it. He is a good God. My failure at the prophetic school became fuel in the fire that led me to seek the presence of Jesus by praying for unusually long periods of time. I would wake up at night and immediately begin praying. I would pray in my car, on my way to work, on breaks, and at lunch. Essentially, anywhere I could pray, I did.

This commitment to prayer cultivated something in my life similar to how Samuel lying next to the Ark of God birthed the reinstitution of the prophetic office in Israel. Looking back, I can now see that as I prayed and ministered to the Lord's presence, I was developing a deeper intimacy with Him; and simultaneously, my destiny was being birthed (see 1 Samuel 3:3-10).

The Lord had enrolled me in the school of the Spirit, and my hunger put me in the position to participate and learn how to walk with His Spirit within my spirit. This schooling was similar to when Moses saw the burning bush. A burning bush was not extraordinary, brush fires are common, as in California in the summertime. But what *was* extraordinary was that the bush kept burning—it wasn't being destroyed as in the natural. The Lord used this phenomenon to get Moses' attention.

Let's take a closer look at Exodus 3. Moses saw that though the bush was on fire, it wasn't being consumed:

> *So Moses thought, "I will go over and see this strange sight—why the bush does not burn up." When the Lord saw that he had gone over to look, God called*

to him from within the bush, "Moses! Moses!" And Moses said, "Here I am" (Exodus 3:3-4 NIV).

Similar to this incident, the supernatural of God is manifesting all around us, but we must be sensitive enough to notice it. Like Moses, we must *go, see, and look!* We must answer when He calls us, "Here I am!" When we perceive heavenly activity and respond, godly supernatural encounters happen.

When Moses went over to see the burning bush and hear what God had to say, He told Moses His plans for His people and how Moses would play a part in those plans. Each sign and wonder that shook Egypt was told to Moses beforehand. Though Moses had received the impartation by being in the presence of God, he had to learn how to trust in the power and the presence of God.

Through God's power all things were and are possible and are signs for others to see and experience.

Then God instructed Moses:

> *Then the Lord said to him, "What is that in your hand?" "A staff," he replied. The Lord said, "Throw it on the ground." Moses threw it on the ground and it became a snake, and he ran from it. Then the Lord said to him, "Reach out your hand and take it by the tail." So Moses reached out and took hold of the snake and it turned back into a staff in his hand. "This," said the Lord, "is so that they may believe that the Lord, the God of their fathers—the God of Abraham, the God of Isaac and the God of Jacob—has appeared to you."*

Then the Lord said, "Put your hand inside your cloak."
So Moses put his hand into his cloak, and when he
took it out, the skin was leprous—it had become as
white as snow. "Now put it back into your cloak," he
said. So Moses put his hand back into his cloak, and
when he took it out, it was restored, like the rest of his
flesh. Then the Lord said, "If they do not believe you
or pay attention to the first sign, they may believe the
second" (Exodus 4:2-8 NIV).

In this Scripture passage from Exodus 4, we see a glimpse of God's school of the Spirit. God is teaching Moses how to operate in the spiritual realm. Without this understanding of the supernatural, Moses would not have been able to accomplish his divine assignment.

GOD INSTRUCTED MOSES, MOSES OBEYED, AND GOD SHOWED MOSES THE POWER OF HIS WORD.

God instructed Moses and Moses obeyed. Then God showed He had the power to back up what He spoke. Much like God imparted His power to Moses, God has imparted many things to His modern-day church. And because of the power of the resurrection, we have greater glory available to us. We actually are the same church that was born in Acts chapter 2, but too many of us are sleeping and/or spiritually unaware. God wants us to be upgraded into notable miracles and greater works—we need to accept the supernatural upgrade God has offered us.

Though other miracles and healings took place at the gathering that day when the young man regained his speech and physical capacity, everyone who speaks to me about that time talks about the man who received a miracle from Jesus. Similar to the days of Elijah when God answered by fire, our generation will be turned upside down by a church of power and demonstration. No agenda from hell can withstand the glory that is rising.

Spiritual Blindness

The school of the Spirit reveals what is right in front of us but we don't see it. For example, when Jesus went to His hometown, people didn't recognize Him as a prophet or the Messiah. They were suffering from "spiritual blindness."

When Jesus traveled to Nazareth, His hometown, He went to the temple and read aloud from the book of Isaiah:

> *The Spirit of the Lord is on me, because he has anointed me to proclaim good news to the poor. He has sent me to proclaim freedom for the prisoners and recovery of sight for the blind, to set the oppressed free, to proclaim the year of the Lord's favor* (Luke 4:18:19 NIV).

When Jesus finished reading, He rolled up the scroll, handed it to the attendant, sat down, and then told those around Him, *"Today this scripture is fulfilled in your hearing"* (Luke 4:21 NIV). In other words Jesus told them that He is the One the Scripture is talking about. He has been sent by God. He is the Messiah.

But they don't believe it. The people said, *"How can this be? …Isn't this Joseph's son?"* (Luke 4:22 NLT). In other words, the people thought that surely God wouldn't pick an ordinary carpenter's son to be the Savior or even a prophet. They were blind to who was right in front of their eyes. Yeshua! The Messiah! The One they had been waiting for!

Jesus tells them matter of factly, *"But I tell you the truth, no prophet is accepted in his own hometown"* (Luke 4:24 NLT). Then Jesus cites the example of Elijah not being sent to his own hometown during a famine; rather, God sent him to a widow in the land of Sidon. The people became furious and came close to pushing Jesus over a cliff, but He walked away right through the threatening crowd (Luke 4:25-30).

The Son of God was in their midst and told them straight out that *"the Spirit of the Lord is upon me,"* and God *"anointed me to bring Good News,"* yet they wanted to get rid of him! They saw Jesus with their physical eyes but didn't recognize who He actually was because they were spiritually blind.

This is why many people even in the Body of Christ today fail to see certain dimensions of the supernatural. Paul's prayer to the church in Ephesus speaks to the need for deep spiritual understanding:

> *Having their understanding darkened, being alienated from the life of God, because of the ignorance that is in them, because of the blindness of their heart* (Ephesians 4:18 NKJV).

In many ways we still dishonor Jesus and miss His move because we are unaware of spiritual matters and don't recognize Jesus. This is why Paul's prayer was for the eyes of their understanding to open. Understanding opens our eyes and hearts to experience the riches of His glory. God wants us to know what is inside us and how His power works so we can use it, and recognize it in operation.

Born-again believers are all filled with the Holy Spirit, but many don't see any power in their lives, even people who sincerely pray and seek God. Why? The culprit is ignorance. The more God reveals to us about the supernatural, the more we can walk in it. This may seem simple, but it's true. One of the most common reasons why we lack the supernatural in our lives—found in the book of Acts, while having the same Holy Spirit—is spiritual blindness. Yes there are other factors, but ignorance is one of the most devious ways the enemy hinders the church from becoming a powerhouse for advancing the Kingdom.

Walking in the Supernatural

What you learn in the school of the Spirit is far greater than any other school, no matter how prestigious. You know you have learned a valuable *spiritual* lesson in the supernatural when you can demonstrate it. God doesn't teach just to fill our heads—He teaches us so we can participate in advancing the Kingdom of God.

It is also important to realize that He uses anointed ministers, the Holy Spirit, Jesus, angels, and even people who are in the great cloud of witnesses to teach us. God often begins by sending a person into your life who can disciple and teach you the ways of the Spirit.

I cannot overstate how important it is to value mentoring types of relationships. Spiritual fathers and mothers can truly accelerate you into the spiritual realm of God. Don't only value what you can get from them, value the person or persons. Honor them. This chapter is not about spiritual parents; but God can use them not just to hold you accountable, but also help birth you into new spiritual understandings or dimensions in God.

Many people think it must have been amazing to be discipled by Jesus. But I wonder why anyone would wonder about that when we have the same opportunity now to be discipled through the Holy Spirit. We are not offered a lesser discipleship. The Spirit and the anointing have been training people since Adam and Eve were in the Garden. The apostles—Matthew, Mark, Luke, and John—were the first to be trained in apostleship; but in the supernatural, many other men and women learned how to walk with God.

Paul is an excellent example of a spiritual father who was taught by the Holy Spirit: *"I want you to know, brothers and sisters, that the gospel I preached is not of human origin. I did not receive it from any man, nor was I taught it; rather, I received it by revelation from Jesus Christ"* (Galatians 1:11-12 NIV).

Just as Paul received the same core training as the other apostles who had physically walked with Jesus, we can also access God's discipleship courses through His Spirit. The Holy Spirit is the best Teacher. The more intimate we become with the Holy Spirit, the more He will reveal Jesus and His Kingdom to us.

The Anointing Teacher

Now let's discuss the teacher called the anointing. Anointing simply means to be made holy or set apart for a special purpose or special ability. For example, David was anointed the king of Israel; Elijah anointed Hazael as king; the Holy Spirit anointed Jesus: *"The Spirit of the Lord is upon me...He has anointed me to..."* (see Isaiah 61; Luke 4).

The apostle John tells us:

> *But the anointing which you have received from Him abides in you, and you do not need that anyone teach you; but as the same anointing teaches you concerning all things, and is true, and is not a lie, and just as it has taught you, you will abide in Him* (1 John 2:27 NKJV).

The anointing inside you will teach you all things. What I love about the anointing is that it doesn't teach aimlessly. The specific anointing you have will teach you how to use it. The prophetic anointing will teach you about the prophetic world. The healing anointing will teach you about healing ministry, and so on.

Much like natural school, there are foundations we all must learn. For example, we learn colors and shapes before we learn how to read words, and this is the same for everyone no matter what career path we take in life.

In the spiritual realm when we are saved, we all begin learning the same elementary principles. His anointing will protect us from false teaching and begin to teach us specifically what we need to know for our particular calling. When we are ready, we are moved from general studies into schooling to prepare us for our divine major.

I will use the prophetic as an example. All of God's people are called to be prophetic, but this doesn't mean that all believers will go through the same degree of training as a fivefold office prophet.

The anointing will even lead and guide you to other ministers who carry the insight, revelation, and wisdom you need for their calling. For example, someone can sit and listen to two preachers and gravitate more toward one than the other because of the preacher's anointing. There have been times when I have listened to a particular minister and in that season I was not ready for what he was teaching—only to hear that teaching again later and be amazed at all I received from it.

Graduation Fruits

As students attending the school of the Spirit, we gain a foundation and then progressively develop until we reach graduation. True discipleship is not intended to produce something different from what was produced in the early church. When we are truly being discipled, the end result will be when we walk as manifested—fully vested and fruitful in our faith—sons and daughters on earth. Without God's discipleship system involving Jesus, angels, fivefold equippers, the great cloud of witnesses, and the Holy Spirit, the church will never mature into the image or likeness of Christ.

Through the school of the Spirit, I went from being the only person in a class who couldn't prophesy, to someone who sees stage-four cancer healed, blind eyes and deaf ears open, the lame walk, and when waving my hands in the glory, people fall without me touching them. I see biblical deliverances and I travel by visions.

I don't write this to brag—I write it to tell you that the Holy Spirit is the greatest Teacher and He can upgrade your supernatural spiritual abilities according to His will. Your impact on earth as a graduate of the school of the Spirit will be life changing not only for you but for multiple others.

Let's ask the Holy Spirit to enroll us in His supernatural school where we will learn to fulfill our God-given purpose. I encourage you to pray the following prayer and then spend about 30 minutes praying in the Spirit.

Prayer

Father God,

In Jesus' name, I thank You for filling me with Your Spirit. Right now, saturate me in fresh anointing oil and fire, God. I receive the fire of God right now. Light my candle and chase away my darkness. Holy Spirit, You are my Lord and I ask that You come and teach me about Your Kingdom. Train me in Your ways as You taught the prophets of old, the apostles in Scripture, and the people who were filled with Your Spirit in the book of Acts.

Lord, I thank You for the anointing within me, and for teaching me all the things I need to know to fulfill my God-given destiny.

Holy Spirit, right now I ask You to enroll me in the school of the Spirit. I thank You for leading me to apostolic and prophetic leadership that can teach and train me in the ways of the Spirit. Holy Spirit, I thank You that You are my primary Teacher, and I ask that the anointing inside me will teach me everything I need to learn to please You. I pray that You will open Your secrets and mysteries to me, in the name of Jesus.

Father, I'm hungry; but I pray that You give me even more hunger, in the mighty name of Jesus. Lord, prepare me for my destiny. Thank You!

2

ANOTHER PROPHET
LIKE ELIJAH

*See, I will send you another prophet like Elijah
before the coming of the great and dreadful
judgment day of God. His preaching will bring
fathers and children together again, to be of one
mind and heart, for they will know that if they
do not repent, I will come and utterly destroy
their land* (Malachi 4:5-6 Living Bible).

The last words of the book of Malachi tell us that before the great day of the Lord, another prophet like Elijah would come to restore. If we are going to be upgraded supernaturally, we must have insight into the Elijah anointing, the anointing of a prophet.

> *Now Elijah took his mantle, rolled it up, and struck the water; and it was divided this way and that, so that the two of them crossed over on dry ground. …Then he [Elisha] took the mantle of Elijah that had fallen from him, and struck the water, and said, "Where is the Lord God of Elijah?" And when he also had struck the water, it was divided this way and that; and Elisha crossed over* (2 Kings 2:8,14 NKJV).

Elijah's mantle—his anointing as a prophet—was powerful enough to part the waters. Volumes of books can be written on the Elijah anointing; however, I want to focus on why God supernaturally upgraded His church and how that is simply a restoration of what was evident in ancient times.

In Second Kings 6:5 some of Elisha's spiritual sons desired to expand and build a bigger meeting place. As they were building, an ax head they were using fell into the river, in water too deep to retrieve it. This was a predicament because not only did they need the ax, they had borrowed it. So they had lost what belonged to someone else.

> *One day the group of prophets came to Elisha and told him, "As you can see, this place where we meet with you is too small. Let's go down to the Jordan River,*

where there are plenty of logs. There we can build a new place for us to meet." "All right," he told them, "go ahead." "Please come with us," someone suggested. "I will," he said. So he went with them. When they arrived at the Jordan, they began cutting down trees. But as one of them was cutting a tree, his ax head fell into the river. "Oh, sir!" he cried. "It was a borrowed ax!" "Where did it fall?" the man of God asked. When he showed him the place, Elisha cut a stick and threw it into the water at that spot. Then the ax head floated to the surface. "Grab it," Elisha said. And the man reached out and grabbed it (2 Kings 6:1-7 NLT).

Elisha, who was given Elijah's mantle of a prophet's anointing, caused a heavy ax head to float to the top of the water. Wow! This is an example of what is taking place in our day through Elijah's mantle and power. The ax head falling into deep waters could be seen as the mysteries and secrets of the supernatural that God taught to those who were then used mightily by Him.

As we learn these mysteries that the Bible refers to as the knowledge of His glory (Habakkuk 2:14; 2 Corinthians 4:6; Ephesians 1:17; 2 Peter 1:3, 3:18), we will walk in authority and bring revival and awakening to advance God's Kingdom on earth. This knowledge imparted into our spirits will thrust us into the greater works and the supernatural that we read about in the book of Acts.

Divine Recovery of the Lost

There is prophetic significance in the ax head story. God used Elisha to bring divine recovery of what was lost in prophecies to us. We can be anointed in our time with the oil of Elijah to bring rehabilitation and restoration to our generation.

Elijah, Elisha's mentor, raised the dead, multiplied food, commanded natural elements like fire and water, moved in healing, and ran at supernatural speeds in his natural body. In fact, when the hand of God came on him he outran Ahab's chariots! This type of glory and power is inside the bones of the church and are ready to be awakened in this hour.

GLORY AND POWER ARE INSIDE THE CHURCH'S BONES—READY TO BE AWAKENED IN THIS HOUR.

It is important to understand that this ancient oil is for today. So let's continue to connect the dots.

In Luke 9, Jesus transfigures and Elijah and Moses are beside Him. What a wonderful description of Jesus emanating light and actually glistening: *"As He prayed, the appearance of His face was altered, and His robe became white and glistening. And behold, two men talked with Him, who were Moses and Elijah"* (Luke 9:29-30 NKJV).

With that image in mind, I want to point out another heavenly experience. Here Zechariah describes a heavenly experience—he sees a golden lampstand with two olive trees beside it:

> *Now the angel who talked with me came back and wakened me, as a man who is wakened out of his sleep. And he said to me, "What do you see?" So I said, "I am looking, and there is a lampstand of solid gold with a bowl on top of it, and on the stand seven lamps with seven pipes to the seven lamps. Two olive trees are by it, one at the right of the bowl and the other at its left"* (Zechariah 4:1-3 NKJV).

The following is another heavenly experience of the same vision that is found in the book of Revelation. One is prophetic symbolism and the other is actual. The two witnesses are referred to as olive trees and candlesticks:

> *"And I will give power to my two witnesses, and they will prophesy one thousand two hundred and sixty days, clothed in sackcloth." These are the two olive trees and the two lampstands standing before the God of the earth* (Revelation 11:3-4 NKJV).

I believe that these three Scriptures found in Luke, Zechariah, and Revelation tell us what God is speaking to us today—that we are called to walk in the fullness of what is revealed in the Bible.

Throughout the book of Hebrews the Bible says that for those who have gone before us, faith is not complete without us. This means we are still connected. To this day we are still connected to those we read about in the Scriptures. This also means that what they began, others after them will finish.

In First Kings chapter 19 we read about Elijah running away and traveling to Mount Sinai, the mountain of God where he was hiding from Jezebel who wanted to kill him. Then he heard the voice of God tell him:

"Go back the same way you came, and travel to the wilderness of Damascus. When you arrive there, anoint Hazael to be king of Aram. Then anoint Jehu grandson of Nimshi to be king of Israel, and anoint Elisha son of Shaphat from the town of Abel-meholah to replace you as my prophet."...So Elijah went and found Elisha son of Shaphat plowing a field. There were twelve teams of oxen in the field, and Elisha was plowing with the twelfth team. Elijah went over to him and threw his cloak across his shoulders and then walked away (1 Kings 19:15-16,19 NLT)

This means that Elisha was to carry on Elijah's ministry and occupy the same spiritual sphere of influence. Elijah cast his mantle on Elisha and then began the process of training him.

In the supernatural, when we have been chosen to carry a mantle, we are often drawn by the mantle itself on a person. Oftentimes, the people we gravitate toward help us identify the anointing in which we are to walk.

Elijah did train Elisha, but that is where he stopped. He never anointed the other two people, Hazael or Jehu. Elisha would later anoint them. Elisha's anointing of Jehu led to Jezebel being overthrown, and the house of Ahab being completely abolished. When we rise up in the Elijah anointing, we finish appointments that previous generations did not.

Elisha

As we receive from our faith-filled ancestors, we will be like Elisha and recover things of the spirit that have been lost—perhaps even borrowed ax heads. What operated at any time in history to advance God's Kingdom can be revived today. The anointing continued to live in Elisha's bones after his death (see 2 Kings 13:21). We can tap into these ancient anointings still today.

The Anointing Continues

In 2019 I attended a meeting in Dallas, Texas, where there were about eighty hungry people gathered to seek the face of God. As we cried out, time seemed to vanish. Though we were in prayer for more than sixteen hours within two days, I couldn't tell what time it was. It seemed that every minute that passed we were lifted into another realm of glory. The atmosphere was electric and every sound seemed to be inspired by the Holy Spirit—creating a divine symphony. Every shout, every tongue, and even every person's movement seemed to be weighty and supernatural.

Both days were phenomenal, but the second day was unforgettable. I had no idea that God was going to give me something from a different time in history. As we prayed and worshipped, I struggled to stand. As this took place, the apostle hosting the prayer meeting looked at me and began to prophesy what he saw in the spirit happening to me. He said, "I see angels—these are the angels from previous revivals. Chazdon, an angel just threw a mantle on you, the mantle of A.A. Allen."Then I fell down under the power of the prophetic word spoken to me.

I remember sleeping that night covered in fire and glory. This happened on a Saturday, and I had to return to our ministry in Jacksonville, Florida, to preach the next day. On Sunday when my wife and I stepped into our church, people could feel the presence of God. Something was different. Beginning that Sunday, the miracle realm of glory began to flow at a very high level.

We saw a woman's eye open who had been blind in that eye since birth. Doctors had performed two surgeries that failed. Yet that day in church she was healed in the revival of the glory atmosphere. Many others in the room fell under the weight of God's presence. Words can't fully describe what we witnessed.

I'm not saying that I'm special. I'm honestly humbled by how the Lord chooses to use me. One of A.A. Allen's last prophetic words was about how his anointing that resided in Miracle Valley was on the corporate Body of Christ.

Greater Glory Global Revival

Since my encounter in Dallas and the prophecy, we have seen blind eyes open, deaf ears open, stage-four cancer healed, tumors dissolve, the lame walk, and other creative miracles. I believe that this is what will take place in the Body of Christ on a far greater scale. We will see the latter and the former rain fall at the same time. We are at the helm of a greater glory revival as a global body.

Every revival in history was the restoration of ancient spiritual manifestations to the modern-day church. The church is about to have its ax head restored! Though we know that Elijah's mantle is not the only one on earth, I believe his is the mantle of end-time revival—and why its operation signifies, as many have said, the second coming of Jesus as well. The operation of someone with the spirit of Elijah paves the way for Jesus' return.

Many people say that revival is not necessary and they get tired of hearing people talk about it. I do believe that at times there are many people who exaggerate and even pervert the true nature and DNA of revival. Remember that revival sets the stage for the return of Jesus, because during revival a restoration takes place in the church.

I don't preach revival because it's trendy. I preach revival because it's the very nature of the message of the Kingdom. When the early church preached Jesus and His Kingdom, revival was the result.

Revival is evidence that Jesus is closer to returning. The return of Jesus goes hand and hand with revival:

> *Repent therefore and be converted, that your sins may be blotted out, so that times of refreshing may come from the presence of the Lord, and that He may send Jesus Christ, who was preached to you before, whom heaven must receive until the times of restoration of all things, which God has spoken by the mouth of all His holy prophets since the world began* (Acts 3:19-21 NKJV).

When times of refreshing are mentioned, the Lord shall send Jesus. Many people don't understand that there is a direct connection between the final move of God and Jesus returning.

There is a generation that will see the final move of God and Christ's return. The book of Daniel in the Bible gives us insight about revival and awakening before Christ returns. The context of the end times is actually not about the antichrist—yet it's not that the antichrist has no relevance. I just believe that the context of the last days is the outpouring of His Spirit on earth. I also believe that ministries that are not contending for the move of God in their generation in their own unique expressions lack the heart of God. We have to ask ourselves, "If we don't exist to see and move with God, why does our ministry exist? What else is there to do?"

The Bible says that the heavens will withhold Jesus until the restoration of all things:

> *Then times of refreshment will come from the presence of the Lord, and he will again send you Jesus, your appointed Messiah. For he must remain in heaven until the time for the final restoration of all things, as God promised long ago through his holy prophets* (Acts 3:20-21 NLT).

The divine restoration that the Elijah anointing, the prophetic anointing, brings is a major part of preparing the sons and daughters of God for the day the heavens no longer have to withhold Jesus. Before that time, the Body of Christ will see the stirring up of ancient anointings. These anointings and mantles will be awakened; but in order to function in them, we must receive training by the Spirit and through those who operate in them.

Spiritual Mentors

Elisha witnessed Elijah's life and learned from his mentor; otherwise Elisha would not have known how to flow in the power of the anointing. We can see this handing over of the mantle with Joshua and Moses as well. Joshua observed Moses throughout the years of journeying and witnessed first-hand the relationship between Moses and the God of glory, which prepared him to walk in the impartation and mantle he received from Moses.

Even when Moses spent forty days and nights on the mountain in God's glory, Joshua followed his mentor halfway up the mountain, as far as possible. The success Joshua had in crossing over into the Promised Land can be linked to Joshua's relationship with Moses. Moses led God's people to the edge of the Promised Land, and Joshua learned enough from Moses to lead the people the remainder of the way.

If God gives you an assignment and you don't have anyone to observe and/or disciple you in the ways of God, oftentimes, discovering His ways will take longer. But, of course, the Holy Spirit is always willing to reveal His ways and will when you ask.

The disciples were accelerated into the supernatural world through the discipleship of Jesus, which included observing Jesus within the Holy Spirit. Consider Peter walking on the water after he witnessed Jesus do it.

In the three years the apostles walked with Jesus, they began demonstrating supernatural signs and wonders that had been lost for over four hundred years. The silence between the book of Malachi and Matthew was due to no prophets proclaiming and pointing the way to God through the supernatural. Somewhere during that time, the ways of the Spirit were lost. But in God's mercy and grace, the birth and life of Jesus restored an abundance of the supernatural!

John the Baptist

Let's also look at the anointing in operation in the life of John the Baptist and how he prepared people for the only authentic way into the spiritual realm—a real relationship with God our Father through Jesus Christ the Son of God.

Can you imagine hearing John the Baptist's declaration? The glory of God on his voice shook Israel, and people began to gravitate to the strange man preaching in the wilderness. But what did he actually say? He prophesied, *"Repent, for the kingdom of heaven is at hand!"* (Matthew 3:2 NKJV).

In my years of hearing this statement, it never seemed very profound or even prophetic—until I considered the four hundred years of silence and no move of God. Between Malachi and Matthew there is no documentation of any heavenly activity on earth.

According to Scripture, nothing prophetically significant happened. This silence may have shaped a mentality that God and His world were distant and not accessible. Their only model of anything spiritual was men bound by a dead, religious spirit. When Jesus described these men, He called them "blind leaders" and people who had the keys of the Kingdom, but shut the doors of Heaven (Matthew 15:14). Israel found itself disconnected from the spirit realm for generations. They had lost the ways of the Spirit and God's spiritual truths were replaced with human doctrines. Can you imagine going that long without an encounter with the glory of God?

This was the type of mentality that John the Baptist spoke into. He was announcing that Heaven was within reach to a people who had only heard the stories of how God had moved in the past—not during their time. So when John thundered these words, it shook the religious mindset of the day. And when Jesus began His ministry, the early church walked in divine access and world-changing power. They knew they were experiencing Heaven on earth—that it wasn't some far-away, cold place.

I believe God wants you to know that Heaven is within your reach today. I believe this generation needs to know that we can touch Heaven and Heaven can touch us. Our God is not dead. Yes, He is the God of Elijah and Abraham and Moses and Adam—but He is also your God. And He still answers by fire. The fire of Heaven will turn this generation toward the burning bush and the Man who walked on water. The revival of the glory of God in the church will be what transforms backslidden nations that have fallen away from Jesus.

"REPENT, FOR THE KINGDOM OF HEAVEN IS AT HAND!"

This message John the Baptist preached was so essential that Jesus also prophetically declared it as well: *"From that time Jesus began to preach and to say, 'Repent, for the kingdom of heaven is at hand'"* (Matthew 4:17 NKJV). And Matthew 3:17 (NKJV) tells us that after Jesus was baptized and the Holy Spirit settled on Him, a voice from Heaven declared, *"This My beloved Son, in whom I am well pleased."*

In Luke 10:8-11 (NIV), Jesus sends the disciples out to spread the Good News, and he tells them to declare this same message:

> *When you enter a town and are welcomed, eat what is offered to you. Heal the sick who are there and tell them, "The kingdom of God has come near to you." But when you enter a town and are not welcomed, go into its streets and say, "Even the dust of your town we wipe from our feet as a warning to you. Yet be sure of this: The kingdom of God has come near."*

As they declared the message that the Kingdom of Heaven was near, the manifestation of God's glory covered the cities that received them. Every place that responded was saturated in supernatural dimensions of Heaven. That's the kind of glory I want to see upon cities and regions again!

It matters whom you allow to lead you. Too many believers are led by people who are blind to the spiritual realm. Jesus warned the people of His day to disregard the leaders who were disconnected and ignorant of the supernatural. We need to learn the ways of old, to revive the spiritual in our lives. God's ways and His promises are not defunct or "old school." Supernatural realities are eternal and have existed before the foundation of this world—and exist today as well.

God created the natural world to be governed by His fundamental ways or "ancient paths" as the Bible calls them.

> *This is what the Lord says: "Stand at the crossroads and look; ask for the ancient paths, ask where the good way is, and walk in it, and you will find rest for your souls..."* (Jeremiah 6:16 NIV).

You could say these fundamentals "make the world go round." Our natural lives cannot truly change without realizing there are mysteries of God that can only be understood from a supernaturally spiritual perspective. Common Scriptures actually cite these paths, such as Psalm 23 (NKJV) where David mentions how the Lord is his Shepherd who leads him *"in the paths of righteousness."*

Apostles and prophets are called to restore people to the basic realities of God's destiny for them, such as Moses and Elijah did. The Elijah anointing restores all things. This is why Elijah and Moses show up in the New Testament (see Matthew 17:1-3). Their anointings will restore God's people in the old ways—but with the wisdom of all ages, which lead to supernatural upgrades in your spiritual life.

The apostolic and prophetic anointings have not changed from the time of the Bible. Whenever the true nature of these anointings is realized, biblical Christianity comes alive. Strong moves of God embrace the apostolic and prophetic anointing. The apostolic mantle produced miracles and raw power surged from the very operation of this gift through the church.

Now I ask, "Where is the apostolic authority and ancient glory that gave witness to the resurrection of Jesus in a hostile time? Where are the prophets who speak into the spiritual realm and creation itself obeys?"

In Scripture, when nations needed to be revived, or come back to God, He would anoint and raise up apostles and prophets. These two ministry giftings do not exist outside of the context of revival. If we closely examine the book of Acts, revival was at its height when the apostolic was in its rightful place. Apostles are born for revival. Prophets called whole nations to repentance; the very essence of apostolic and prophetic people is the spirit of revival.

Why does the apostolic exist? It doesn't exist to start nice churches, no. It exists to overthrow demonic powers to bring in a harvest of new souls and establish the culture of the Kingdom. Prophets do not exist to speak platitudes to make us feel warm and fuzzy. The word of the Lord in their mouth was meant to initiate Heaven's affairs into our world. When you disconnect a movement from its original purpose, it dies. God is calling forth revivalists. Will you answer the call to be one of them?

The Lord is continuing to awaken the apostolic and prophetic nature of the church. As crises arise in the world, we will see the inevitable rise of an apostolic/prophetic people. Though God has only called some to the offices of apostles and prophets. The Good News is that all of God's people can carry the spirit and power of Elijah through the impartations of these two offices—apostle and prophet. You are called to be an Elisha, one who ushers in restoration!

Prayer

My glorious Father,

Right now in the name of Jesus I pray that You would give me the spirit and power of Elijah. I pray that you would anoint me for these last days. I'm hungry to see revival! I pray that You would revive Your deeds, revive Your works, and let there be restoration of the things of old that we need today. I pray in the name of Jesus that in my life I would see an awakening of the spiritual gifts You have put inside me—and make me another prophet like Elijah.

Father, let there be a divine recovery. Lord Jesus, I have read about how You have used many generals in the past and, God, I'm hungry for those type of prophets and leaders in this time. Lord Jesus, I ask that the mantles of those You used mightily in the past will be taken up by Your sons and daughters today. Release Your glory on earth and help us pick up the mantle like Elisha did so You can transform this generation. In Jesus' name, amen.

3

ACTIVATED BY FIRE

I [John the Baptist] *indeed baptize you with
water unto repentance, but He who is coming
after me is mightier than I, whose sandals I am
not worthy to carry. He will baptize you with the
Holy Spirit and fire* (Matthew 3:11 NKJV).

"Revival! Awakening!" These were the words I heard God
thunder in my spiritual ears one morning as I was half sleep
and half awake. Though the words were simple, they were like
fire in my bones. His words were loaded with supernatural

communication; I didn't realize they would forever change everything about our marriage and life together. That prophetic encounter with the voice of God became the very DNA of our ministry.

After that encounter with God, Emily and I never preached the same again. There was a fresh fire in our ministry and everything changed as we embraced a new assignment to be part of the coming revival and awakening. It sounds cliche, but we really were never the same. We had been baptized by revival fire and His words activated us. We were baptized by revival fire. Lord, I pray that You would baptize all believers in the Holy Spirit and fire!

In Psalm 18:28 (NKJV) David wrote, *"You will light my lamp; the Lord my God will enlighten my darkness."* Through this Psalm we gain insight into how fire activates us into the way and will of God. Directly after, David gives us the results of the fire of God being activated in his life. David writes that the fire that burned in his spirit led to him running through a troop and leaping over a wall (Psalm 18:29). In other words, God's fire manifested supernatural abilities in warfare. David was experiencing what happens when our spirits are activated.

OUR SPIRIT BECOMES ONE WITH THE HOLY SPIRIT.

From Scripture, we know that a human is a three-part being—our full humanity consists of spirit, soul, and then our body (see 1 Thessalonians 5:23). The Bible also tells us that we are made in the image and likeness of God (see Genesis 1:26). This includes our spirit.

One day as I was praying, the Lord said, "Your spirit was made in the image and likeness of the Holy Spirit." At first this offended me because I had only considered the Scripture verse literally, *"Then God said, 'Let Us make man in Our image, according to Our likeness....'"* But then I came to understand that we are made in the image of the Triune God—God the Father, Jesus the Son, and the Holy Spirit. This is why David's prayer of acknowledgement of God's fire led to him operate above natural limitations. We must understand our spirit becoming one with the Holy Spirit.

Toward the end of this chapter, I explain the spirit's similarity to the lamp of God that represents the Holy Spirit. Before we go into detail about the fire of God, I want to briefly explain the human spirit so we understand why the enemy works so hard to extinguish our fire.

Our Human Spirit

From the moment of your salvation, the enemy has bombarded you with religious people who have tried to quench your fire. They make comments such as, "I've been saved longer than you and it doesn't involve any of that supernatural stuff." Or even preachers can be used by the enemy at times to subtlety preach discouragement to put out the flame of God in your life. In this chapter, I pray you will discover a few new dynamics of your spirit that confirm why you must constantly receive fresh fire.

For You will light my lamp; the Lord my God will enlighten my darkness. For by You I can run against a troop, by my God I can leap over a wall (Psalm 18:28-29 NKJV).

The human spirit carries the divine nature of God within it. When we were born again, it was our spirit that was reborn by the DNA of the Father. Our soul will be renewed by the word of God over time as we grow in our relationship to the Lord.

Our physical bodies will be redeemed fully at the return of Jesus (see John 6:40; Romans 8:23; 1 Thessalonians 4:14-17). When we accept Jesus as our Savior, our spirit is instantly born again in babe form. Though we must mature, our growth is not connected to time. In the supernatural realm the past, present, and future all operate simultaneously. Thus, growth is not time regulated like it is in the natural world.

Revelation Knowledge

You may have accepted Jesus twenty years ago, but your spirit could still be a babe due to *a lack of:* 1) time in the presence of God; 2) receiving revelation knowledge; and 3) having encounters with God. Let's look at each of these points.

1. Throughout the Bible we are told to, for example, *"Draw near to God and He will draw near to you"* (James 4:8 NKJV). Prayer brings us into God's presence; and in First Thessalonians 5:16-18 and Psalm 72:15 and Acts 6:4, we are to *"give ourselves continually to prayer"* (NKJV). Praying continually

brings us closer to our heavenly Father—a wonderful place to abide, live, rest, and grow in His ways and will for us.

Praising and worshiping God also brings us into His presence. From Genesis to Revelation, we are admonished to praise and worship our worthy Lord and Savior. In Second Chronicles 7:3 the Bible says, *"When all the people of Israel saw the fire coming down and the glorious presence of the Lord filling the Temple, they fell face down on the ground and worshiped and praised the Lord, saying, 'He is good! His faithful love endures forever!'"* (NLT). The entirety of Psalm 150 is punctuated with exclamation marks—that is how exciting and important it is to *"Praise the Lord!"* which brings you into His presence (see also Psalm 149).

The angel sent to the mother of Jesus states in Luke 1:19 (NLT), *"I am Gabriel! I stand in the very presence of God. It was he who sent me to bring you this good news!"* Jesus' sacrifice on the cross allows us to stand confidently in God's presence: *"Because of Christ and our faith in him, we can now come boldly and confidently into God's presence"* (Ephesians 3:12 NLT). Without guilt or shame we can approach the throne of God's presence, *"let us go right into the **presence** of God with sincere hearts fully trusting him. For our guilty consciences have been sprinkled with Christ's blood to make us clean, and our bodies have been washed with pure water"* (Hebrews 10:22 NLT).

2. The Bible tells us that strong meat is for the mature Christian (see 1 Corinthians 3:1-3). This speaks of the role of revelation knowledge in growing our spirit in the ways of God. Believers who are full of the revelation of God grow at an accelerated rate that causes their spirits to grow. As we

surrender ourselves to sit at the feet of Jesus, He will teach us. His teaching will grow us up, similar to how Jesus taught the disciples in the three years when He was ministering.

The revelation of knowledge of the Kingdom that the disciples were exposed to moved them from glory to glory, but also caused them to grow in spiritual stature. Another example of this spiritual growth is seen when Samuel ministered before the ark. His mother would bring him a new coat every year. Many interpret this as him growing in the spirit—and outgrowing his natural, physical state.

Revelation knowledge can be received by individual believers, by a group, and by the church as a whole. Paul, in First Corinthians 14:6 (NLT), is addressing the church in Corinth:

> *Dear brothers and sisters, if I should come to you speaking in an unknown language, how would that help you? But if I bring you a revelation or some special knowledge or prophecy or teaching, that will be helpful.*

Of course the book of Revelation, the last book in the Bible, is full of revelation knowledge for the worldwide church and is best understood when our spirit connects with the Holy Spirit, who inspired that book as well as the whole of God's Word. Revelation 1:1-3 (NKJV) tells us:

> *The Revelation of Jesus Christ, which God gave Him to show His servants—things which must shortly take place. And He sent and signified it by His angel to His servant John, who bore witness to the word of God, and to the testimony of Jesus Christ, to all things*

that he saw. Blessed is he who reads and those who hear the words of this prophecy, and keep those things which are written in it; for the time is near.

3. Next, the Bible gives us another key for spiritual growth through encounters with God. It says that the mature have learned to exercise their spiritual senses. This means that supernatural encounters do play a role in helping us grow— only in encounters with God and when we are walking in the Spirit do our spiritual senses spring into operation.

For too many years some have taught that supernatural encounters don't matter and have no connection with spiritual growth. But I assure you that you can learn more in one moment of glory than you can in a lifetime of study.

This is why First Corinthians 14:29-31 (NIV) says: *"Two or three prophets should speak, and the others should weigh carefully what is said. And if a revelation comes to someone who is sitting down, the first speaker should stop. For you can all prophesy in turn so that everyone may be instructed and encouraged."* The context is not preaching or teaching. It's flowing in the prophetic realm. In other words, we learn and grow as we flow in the supernatural. In the spirit world, doing is eating meat. This is why Jesus says in Luke 22:42, *"Father, if you are willing, take this cup from me; yet not my will, but **yours be done**"* (NIV).

Just as God did *"miracles in the sight of their ancestors in the land of Egypt"* (Psalm 78:12 NIV), we can experience God encounters today as well. For Jesus says to us, *"Very truly I tell you, whoever believes in me will do the works I have been doing, and they will do even greater things than these, because I am going to the Father"* (John 14:12 NIV; see also John 5:20). Today,

God is enabling His children to carry on His supernatural works through encounters with Him.

Are you willing to open your eyes and receive a spiritual upgrade?

Moving With His Spirit

One of the highest dimensions of revelation is accessed by doing God's will and moving with His Spirit. We need His fire to come and move us out of dormancy. Many of us are filled with knowledge about the supernatural. Yet at the same time we haven't peaked in growth because we haven't stepped out with what we have learned to demonstrate it—to bring God glory and advance His Kingdom.

OUR BORN-AGAIN SPIRIT, BEING ALIVE, IS SIGNIFIED BY FIRE—A LIGHT TO DISPEL THE DARKNESS.

Your spirit is the primary part of you and consists of more than just your natural senses. The reason Paul could make statements about being in his body or out of his body concerning God encounters tells us that his spirit and physical body looked the same. The human spirit has an anatomy—it's just invisible. The Bible refers to this spirit part of us as the *"candle of the Lord"* (Proverbs 20:27 King James Version). Much like the seven golden candlesticks represent the Holy Spirit, our spirit is also a candle.

Just like the lamp of God was never to go out, our spirits should never be without fire. Candles are created to bring light. When the fire of a candle goes out, it can no longer do what it was created to do. Our spirit, being alive, is signified by fire.

Let's read a portion of First Samuel chapter 3 where we can see in Scripture what happens when the lamp of God dims and then is extinguished:

> *Now the boy Samuel ministered to the Lord before Eli. And the word of the Lord was rare in those days; there was no widespread revelation. And it came to pass at that time, while Eli was lying down in his place, and when his eyes had begun to grow so dim that he could not see, and before the lamp of God went out in the tabernacle of the Lord where the ark of God was, and while Samuel was lying down, that the Lord called Samuel. And he answered, "Here I am!" …Now the Lord came and stood and called as at other times, "Samuel! Samuel!" And Samuel answered, "Speak, for Your servant hears"* (1 Samuel 3:1-4,10 NKJV).

God was lighting Samuel's candle as the light of his mentor (Eli) was being extinguished (see 1 Samuel 3:12-14). Samuel would mature into a powerful prophet of God:

> *As Samuel grew up, the Lord was with him, and everything Samuel said proved to be reliable. And all Israel, from Dan in the north to Beersheba in the south, knew that Samuel was confirmed as a prophet*

of the Lord. The Lord continued to appear at Shiloh and gave messages to Samuel there at the Tabernacle (1 Samuel 3:19-21 NLT).

In Psalm 74:9 we learn that when the prophets are not functioning, the supernatural is not being experienced: *"We no longer see your miraculous signs. All the prophets are gone, and no one can tell us when it will end"* (Psalm 74:9 NLT).

Fanning the Flames

Where there is no fire, there is no supernatural signs and wonders. If you attend a meeting where there is no fire and then go to one where people are burning, you will notice a totally different demonstration of the Spirit's power.

The apostle Paul told his spiritual son Timothy to *"stir up the gift of God which is in you through the laying on of my hands"* (2 Timothy 1:6 NKJV). This stirring up can be interpreted as fanning the flame of the gifts of the Spirit (see 1 Corinthians 12:1-11). When you operate the gift in you, you light the holy fire of God in your life. Keeping that light bright means operating your gift to the benefit of the Kingdom of God.

Many people have gifts, but they lay dormant. I pray that as you read this, the oil and fire of God would fall upon you and cause a divine stirring in your spirit. God wants to awaken the spirit in you through fire as our spiritual gifts flow through our spiritual senses. Just as when sleeping our senses become dull, our spirits can also slumber. The more awake or alive our spirit is, the more sensitive we are when God interacts with us.

To give an example of our spiritual gifts flowing through our spiritual senses, I want to tell you a story. Many times I've heard people talk about the discerning of spirits through sight. I have certainly had dreams that helped me discern spirits, to see clearly what I was dealing with. However, I have discovered that discerning spirits can flow through any of the five spiritual senses—seeing, hearing, taste, smell, touch. One of the most reliable ways this gift of discerning spirits functions in my life is through the sense of touch.

Spiritual Discernment

This is typically how I discern demon spirits and even demonic agents who are not just demonized people, but people working with satan to bring others down. At times these gifts may activate while I'm ministering or while in normal interactions with people such as shaking hands.

One Sunday when I was laying hands on people during an altar call. I reached out to touch a young man who was from a different country. When I touched him, I felt a cold, unclean presence. The sensation was quick and cold. I am very familiar with this feeling because as a child I was tormented by night terrors. All my hair would stand up, and I could feel witchcraft spirits, but didn't know what they were. I believe this may be why God uses me to discern demonic spirits. It's a language I understand.

Instantly I knew this young man was not just demonized by witchcraft—he was actually involved in it. He was even trying to join critical parts of the ministry and giving large monetary seeds weekly to gain favor. My touch discernment and his motives to connect with our ministry were all red flags, which prompted me to give him no influence in our ministry. He soon left without causing damage.

I OFTEN FEEL A MANTLE OF FIRE, GLORY, OR POWER BEING DRAPED AROUND ME.

Another example of spiritual discernment is when I had just finished preaching and was resting in the pastor's office where I had ministered. A friend of his came and asked if he could prophesy over me. I agreed and he reached out to touch me. The moment he did, the discerning of spirits gift began to function and I felt the presence of a demon spirit. I immediately knew not to receive the words he was speaking.

Before I preach on the road, I often feel a mantle of fire, glory, or power being draped around me. This type of covering is discerning of spirits, and at the same time it's my sense of touch interacting with the spirit realm.

When you receive prayer at an altar and feel a sensation and go down, that is your spiritual sense of touch sensing whatever is being imparted into you. When you are in prayer and begin to feel the presence of God, that is not only because He is manifesting Himself. It's also because your sense of touch is discerning the presence of Jesus, the Holy Spirit, or the angels of God.

Once while I was opening prayer corporately for a service, I was declaring over the congregation, but I didn't feel anything special. There was no strong presence of God that I could sense; and honestly, I didn't feel like I was praying well. Suddenly out of nowhere I had an open-eye vision. In this vision, the room where I was standing began to shake violently. It looked as if I was watching a YouTube video of an earthquake caught by a security camera. My eyes were wide open and I began to prophesy what I was seeing. There was a great move of God that day. We were all shaken because of the activity taking place in the spiritual realm.

Spiritual Activity

These examples reveal that the gifts of the spirit can flow through any of our natural senses to experience spiritual encounters. The more we develop our spiritual senses, the more we will flow in the Spirit. But we can't forget that our spirit's condition can determine how deep into the supernatural we go.

Revelation 3:18 says that the Laodicia church needed to heal their spiritual eyes with eye salve. The Bible also says in Revelation 3:22 (NIV), *"Whoever has ears, let them hear what the Spirit says to the churches."* This Scripture tells us that people have spiritual ears that can hear the voice of God and the Holy Spirit. People can also be spiritually deaf. I have actually cast out demons that had caused spiritual deafness and blindness, which are our primary senses.

The Bible says that Daniel had an excellent spirit. I used to believe that this meant he did everything well. Then I studied Daniel chapter 5 and realized it meant something different.

Inasmuch as an excellent spirit, knowledge, understanding, interpreting dreams, solving riddles, and explaining enigmas were found in this Daniel, whom the king named Belteshazzar, now let Daniel be called, and he will give the interpretation (Daniel 5:12 NKJV).

This verse describes abilities that Daniel had because his *spirit* was in excellent condition. These abilities included: knowledge, understanding, interpreting dreams, solving mysteries, and explaining and solving problems. All of these were supernatural capabilities due to his spirit being in great condition. Our spirit is key to us walking with God in the supernatural. If we desire to walk with Him as Enoch and many others did, our spirit cannot be in the state of slumber. We must be awakened by fire.

It is no coincidence that our spirit becomes one with the Holy Spirit. It's also not a coincidence that when humankind fell, the part of us that fell and died was the spirit. When Adam's spirit died, God asked, "Where are you?" Why would God, who knows everything, ask that question? It was not because God did not know where Adam was. It was because Adam was no longer connected to Him in the spiritual dimensions.

Our spirits were created to function in the spiritual realm in a similar way to how our natural bodies enable us to function in the natural realm. God wants our spirits to be alive and connected to Him. Awakening is not just an awareness of God. Awakening is when our spirit comes out of slumber, enabling us to walk in the Spirit. God wants to bring revival and awakening to each generation. His fire will awaken the church.

Controversial Spiritual Gifts

Many of the gifts God desires to operate in His church create the most controversy and division. Jesus said, *"I came to send fire on the earth, and how I wish it were already kindled!"* (Luke 12:49 NKJV). This means that Jesus desires His Spirit to fill the earth.

Jesus continues in the next few verses speaking of the division His fire will create. The New Living Translation cites what Jesus says this way:

> *I have come to set the world on fire, and I wish it were already burning! I have a terrible baptism of suffering ahead of me, and I am under a heavy burden until it is accomplished. Do you think I have come to bring peace to the earth? No, I have come to divide people against each other! From now on families will be split apart, three in favor of me, and two against—or two in favor and three against* (Luke 12:49-52 NLT).

On the day of Pentecost when all the believers were meeting together in one place, Peter read Joel's prophecy about the outpouring of God's Spirit (see Acts 2:17-21). We do indeed see dreams, visions, prophesying, signs, and wonders today! And with this in mind, we can see clearly why God's fire creates division. When God's fire comes, the supernatural is activated, which results in division because there is controversy about supernatural manifestations and demonstrations.

The fire of God brings what has been done in Scripture, and it won't bring anything less. Out-of-body experiences, visions, dreams, visitations, glory, signs, creative miracles, multiplication of food and money, people falling under the power, shaking, trembling, angelic activity, strange acts, demons cast out, speaking in tongues, prophesying, demonstrations of the Spirit, miracles in the weather, and more are going to be experienced by those who are baptized in fire. God's presence will be with you and you will know He is God!

> *Then you call on the name of your gods, and I will call on the name of the Lord; and the God who answers by fire, He is God* (1 Kings 18:24 NKJV).

Prayer

Holy Spirit,

I thank You for Your fire. Lord, when You came on the day of Pentecost You submerged the early church in fire and brought them into the fullness of the supernatural. Lord, I am praying that You do the same thing for me. I pray right now that I would not only speak in tongues but that You would submerge me in Your fire, engulf me in Your flame. I pray that right now I would be completely consumed by the fire of God.

Lord, let my candle be set ablaze in the name of Jesus. I pray that every power that would try to extinguish my flame and dry out my spiritual life will be banished. I pray that by the power of the blood of Jesus those evil powers would scatter in Jesus' name. I thank You that when Your fire came that Your church began to move in the supernatural. Right now, Father, let Your fire come and activate me. Let the gifts inside me be stirred right now, let the anointing inside me be stirred right now so I can walk in obedience to Your calling.

Father, I thank You that just as the angel stirred the pools of Bethesda, You are stirring in my spirit right now. I thank You that today I am receiving power to be Your witness, in the name of Jesus. Lord, work through my life the same way You worked through the early church. Set me on fire. In Jesus' name, amen.

4

GOD'S OFFSPRING

For you did not receive the spirit of bondage
again to fear, but you received the Spirit of
adoption by whom we cry out, "Abba, Father."
The Spirit Himself bears witness with our spirit
that we are children of God, and if children, then
heirs—heirs of God and joint heirs with Christ,
if indeed we suffer with Him, that we may also
be glorified together (Romans 8:15-17 NKJV).

"Religion" is dead philosophies and traditions that have hin-
dered many generations of believers from walking in their full

inheritance as children of God. One of the spirit of religion's primary assignments is to warp our view of Jesus in the present. Typically, religious doctrine limits the power of God to only the past and expects the power to return in the future. Religion never puts the power of God into the present; it wants to remove any expectation of miracles, signs, wonders, or any demonstration of God's power. Religious institutions hide the lack of God in their ministry and the lives of their followers. Yet! There is a remnant in this generation who will not be denied our inheritance.

I often laugh at some "Christian" movies. Believers are depicted as weak and the version of Jesus they present to the world is simply not the Jesus of Scripture reality. In the movies He lacks boldness and is not confrontational. The disciples are all elderly, and the Bible is often twisted to enhance the storyline. I don't find any of this a coincidence. I believe satan is afraid of the world encountering the real, resurrected Jesus. He trembles at the thought of God's children gaining true revelation of who Jesus is, so satan fights to keep us believing false opinions of our powerful and almighty Savior.

Another area that religion dilutes is our identity as sons and daughters of God. This reality has been reduced to a title we call ourselves. Many charismatics have embraced who Jesus truly is, but we must continue to grasp why Jesus came to understand fully who we really are. Jesus is called the last Adam because He reclaimed all the legal rights to rule the earth that the first Adam lost when he disobeyed God the Father.

Have you ever considered that as spectacular as the universe is with all its galaxies and numerous stars, moons, planets, and suns, God created humans as His most creative centerpiece. Just think about how complex creation truly is. Yet we are the only beings God created who are made in His image and likeness in the spiritual and the natural world. We hold a place that satan can never have. In fact, satan's fall was because he wanted to be like the Son of Man. This means God made us in the condition and position satan desired to have—but never will. This speaks to why satan hates humans; but more importantly, it speaks of humankind's significance.

The First Adam and the Last Adam

Let's take a moment to ponder the similarities between the first Adam and the last Adam. Both were dressed in glory, given rulership, and had an assignment to expand God's Kingdom. It's easy to read about the first Adam (see Genesis chapters 2–4) and miss something undeniable. Both the first and the last Adam reveal God's intent for humankind. In fact, seeing Jesus gives us insight into who Adam was *before* the fall—when Adam and Eve chose to disobey God and severed their spiritual bond with their heavenly Father.

The first Adam had a miraculous birth—He was created solely by God (see Genesis 2:7). Likewise, the last Adam was conceived miraculously. Jesus' birth was God's way to release pure DNA that was without sin. Jesus was not born in sin because His DNA did not come from anyone who had a sinful nature. Jesus received the Father's DNA and He received His body from Mary, a virgin. Likewise was Adam, before the fall.

Then Adam sinned and Jesus was sent by God to return us to the fullness of life.

Jesus came to the earth and emptied Himself of all divinity. He was 100 percent human. This is why no miracles took place in His life until after He was filled with the Holy Spirit. Jesus showed us what a human in the right relationship with the Father can be, which is what Adam and Eve were *before* the fall.

Everything Jesus did on earth was as a man. He was completely dependent on the fullness of the Holy Spirit. Jesus lived a holy life, walked on water, rebuked storms, raised the dead, healed the sick, cast out devils, died on the cross, and was raised from the dead—all as a man.

Jesus lived as a human because the Creator God gave humankind dominion over the earth. He could not defeat death as God within the earth's domain. When God spoke over the first Adam that he had rulership in the earth, it was final. God's words over Adam were not just to him as an individual. God's word released purpose over the entire kind, which is why satan needed to gain influence over Adam. With that influence, satan could rule the earth throughout every generation because of the authority God gave the first Adam.

HUMANS HAVE THE GOD-GIVEN RESPONSIBILITY TO CARE FOR HIS CREATION.

God gave humankind dominion, or the responsibility for His creation, saying, "*So God created man in His own image; in the image of God He created him; male and female He created them. Then God blessed them, and God said to them, 'Be fruitful and multiply; fill the earth and subdue it; have dominion...'*" (Genesis 1:27-29 NKJV). When God made everything in Genesis, He spoke creation into existence.

When reading the creation history recorded in Genesis 1 and 2, we can see a significant shift after God created man. After this delegation of authority from God to Adam, God placed Adam in the Garden and commanded him not to eat from the tree of the knowledge of good and evil (see Genesis 2:15-18). Then Adam named the animals. So it went from God speaking and creating, to man speaking to creation. The earth was made to be governed, regulated, and influenced by the children of God. When they veer from the path of righteousness, as they have done throughout the centuries, consequences await.

The Savior Adam

When Jesus defeated death, He became the firstborn of many siblings: "*For God knew his people in advance, and he chose them to become like his Son, so that his Son would be the firstborn among many brothers and sisters*" (Romans 8:29 NLT). Man could not be born again until Jesus defeated death. There is a direct link to the new birth and Jesus' resurrection. This is why in the Gospel of John, Jesus talks about the Holy Spirit.

The temple veil that separated people from God's presence was torn in half when Jesus died. The torn veil symbolizes that once again—as was in the Garden of Eden before the fall, people would have access to the presence of God. This access also allows the Holy Spirit to dwell in our human hearts.

In the Old Testament, prophets were referred to as servants, because without the new birth—being filled with the Spirit—they could be anointed, but they weren't born of water and spirit so they could not be considered sons or daughters of God.

> *So you have not received a spirit that makes you fearful slaves. Instead, you received God's Spirit when he adopted you as his own children. Now we call him, "Abba, Father." For his Spirit joins with our spirit to affirm that we are God's children. And since we are his children, we are his heirs. In fact, together with Christ we are heirs of God's glory...* (Romans 8:15-17 NLT).

When we are born again, we have received an incorruptible seed, the exact seed that caused Jesus to be born without sin. Your new birth was nothing short of miraculous. Being newborn sons and daughters of God makes us beloved *offspring of God.* This is why the Pharisees said Jesus was a blasphemer when He said that He was the Son of God. In ancient Jewish culture, a son inherited his father's profession. So to be the Son of God was to call yourself God.

When the Pharisees questioned Jesus about this, He said in John 10:34 (NKJV), *"...Is it not written in your law, 'I said, "You are gods."'"* Jesus never denied it. So, for shock value I could say that Christians could be classified as a God-breed of people. We are people who have become the offspring of God and inherited the divine essence of who He is. We are younger siblings of our big Brother, Jesus. That is the truth mere religion—religion without the presence of God, forms of godliness without power—does not want us to know. It seems to many that this family relationship places humans too high, too close to Father God.

The Family of God

But I want to challenge your thinking about your relationship with your heavenly Father. It's time to come out of low thinking about yourself. In Ephesians, the Bible gives insight about what takes place when the eyes of our heart open and we begin to understand the glorious inheritance inside us. God wants us to have a revelation of Him, as well as what He put in our spirit when we are born again. (See First 1 John 3:1-2; Matthew 5:9; John 1:12; Romans 8:14,17; Galatians 3:26; Ephesians 5:1; Philippians 2:15.)

We must simply agree with the Scriptures—trusting God's Word. We have been seated in heavenly places with Christ and we are joint heirs. Jesus, our elder Brother, joyfully shares His inheritance with us. This truth is why He was crucified; it was not the miracles or the demonstrations of God's power, though these things ruffled feathers—it was that He said He was the Son of God that truly upset the religious officials. Consider what was said in Matthew as Jesus stood before the Sanhedrin:

Then the high priest stood up and said to Jesus, "Well, aren't you going to answer these charges? What do you have to say for yourself?" But Jesus remained silent. Then the high priest said to him, "I demand in the name of the living God—tell us if you are the Messiah, the Son of God." Jesus replied, "You have said it. And in the future you will see the Son of Man seated in the place of power at God's right hand and coming on the clouds of heaven." Then the high priest tore his clothing to show his horror and said, "Blasphemy! Why do we need other witnesses? You have all heard his blasphemy. What is your verdict?" "Guilty!" they shouted. "He deserves to die!" (Matthew 26:62-65 NLT)

What was Jesus guilty of? He was guilty of admitting the truth—that He was the Son of Man, the Messiah.

We share in Jesus' death as we die to self and pick up the cross. We share in "His sufferings that we may share in His glory."

The same authority that the first Adam had is available now. This truth is widely fought against—nevertheless, it is the missing link between obtaining our inheritance here and now. This truth is extremely offensive to people who are not born again; but when you become a child of God, nothing about you is ordinary anymore. You defy logic and reason. You blur the line between possible and impossible.

Remember, Romans 8:17 says that we are joint heirs with Christ. This is an extremely powerful position in God's family, because heirs are people legally entitled to the property or rank of another upon that person's death. This was the shift from the Old Covenant to the New. We went from servants to children, making us partakers of the inheritance passed from the Father to His heirs.

MANY BELIEVERS DON'T EMBRACE THE FACT THAT THEY ARE PARTAKERS IN CHRIST'S DIVINE NATURE.

One main reason this truth isn't accepted by believers is because they don't embrace that they are now partakers in Christ's divine nature. A major shift takes place when people go from believing that God is supernatural to believing that they too are supernatural as we come from God's actual lineage.

In my wife's book, *The Blueprint: An Intercessor's Guide for Effective Prayer*, Emily explains our relationship with our Father as sons and daughters. It is a powerful revelation. It is also a revelation that is needed so we can see God as our Father. The following is an excerpt from the book:

> God is our Heavenly Father. Over time in my walk, I have come to find that many have such a hard time seeing God as Father. Some say it is how they were raised; stating "He is Jehovah God and because of that He does not play games with you." For others I have found that they never had a relationship with their earthly father to even get an understanding of God as a Father. I am sure

there are many other reasons too, but I want to stop there so we can move on and get into this God equals Father business.

As the Lord broke down His prayer to me, He first said, "They must know me as Father." That blew my mind because it is literally the first thing you state in the Lord's prayer…Our Father. You cannot move on to the next part of prayer without first knowing Him as your Father. It is a vital foundation too if you take the time to think about it. Let me explain what I mean.

When you have a natural father, you have no issue going to him to ask for pretty much anything. When I was a little girl, I would run to my dad asking for things. Not as a spoiled child, but as a loved child, who knew my daddy loved me and would give me the world if he could. That is a true relationship. A child goes to their parents because they know that they are there to take care of them. My father and mother supplied my needs, and I was confident in that knowledge.

There were times my dad would tell me no, but that never stopped me from coming to him for anything I wanted or needed. I was never afraid to ask him, and his "no" never left me feeling rejected. I watch my children do the same with their daddy and I am confident that they know my husband would do anything he could to make them happy. He would try and lasso the moon to see a smile on their faces. Going above and beyond for your kids is just what parents do.

This is how the Father wants us to see Him. Excited and eager for us, His children, to ask Him for anything. He wants us to know Him as a loving, doting, and devoted Father, who wants to put a smile on our faces. Will He always say yes? No, absolutely not, but that is the best part of having a Father who loves you unconditionally. He will say no to teach you things. Always remember we are to be loved not spoiled.

Abba Father is not what the world has defined nor even redefined a father to be. He is, always has been, and always will be greater than what we can even comprehend as father. We can no longer use what the world prescribes us because it is tainted. It is fashioned from negativity for negativity. We must be wiser and learn to "taste and see that the Lord is good" (Psalm 34:8 NIV). I say find out for yourself what kind of Father God is, and you be the judge if what He gives is a thousand times better than what you have known. No one can out-father the BEST Father.

5

The Human Spirit

It's impossible to talk about sons and daughters and separate its true meaning from the supernatural. The radical rise of the glory in the earth is connected to the church uncovering the hidden mystery of Jesus and also the glorious inheritance inside the saints. The eyes of our understanding must be opened to fully comprehend the glorious inheritance we have within us—which is exactly Paul's prayer for the Ephesians:

I have not stopped giving thanks for you, remembering you in my prayers. I keep asking that the God of our Lord Jesus Christ, the glorious Father, may give you the Spirit of wisdom and revelation, so that you may know him better. I pray that the eyes of your heart may be enlightened in order that you may know the hope to which he has called you, the riches of his glorious inheritance in his holy people, and his incomparably great power for us who believe. That power is the same as the mighty strength (Ephesians 1:16-19 NIV).

Notice that Paul prayed for the Spirit of wisdom and revelation in the knowledge of Jesus, and also he prayed that we would realize who we are.

The Bible says that those who are partakers of the Holy Spirit will have a "foretaste" of the power of the age to come:

And we believers also groan, even though we have the Holy Spirit within us as a foretaste of future glory, for we long for our bodies to be released from sin and suffering. We, too, wait with eager hope for the day when God will give us our full rights as his adopted children, including the new bodies he has promised us… (Romans 8:23 NLT).

I can confidently say that power from the future glory world does not look like the average churchgoer. Without question, it will look like people being healed in someone's shadow and/or people being translated without knowing if they are in their physical body or not. For us to comprehend what it means to be born again, we must first embrace God as our Father and the fact that we are His very offspring. Let's take a moment to delve into this experience.

The Born-Again Experience

When you were born again, the part of you that was born was your spirit. We can't talk about being children of God without discussing the part of us that was regenerated at the new birth through God's Spirit and incorruptible seed. This is the part of you that died when Adam and Eve ate the fruit. After they ate the God-forbidden fruit from the tree of the knowledge of good and evil, God asked, "Adam, where are you?"

As mentioned previously, this question is intriguing because God already knows where Adam is. God is all knowing. What then, is the deeper meaning of the question? When Adam's spirit died because of disobedience, the part of him that was designed for the supernatural world was disconnected from it. Consequently God was referring to Adam's spiritual disconnection from Him.

The Holy Spirit comes alive in us when we are born again. At that born-again time we are connected or joined to God's Spirit. After a new birth we become one with His Spirit:

> *But whoever is united* [joined] *with the Lord is one with him in spirit* (1 Corinthians 6:17 NIV).
>
> *But you are not controlled by your sinful nature. You are controlled by the Spirit if you have the Spirit of God living in you. (And remember that those who do not have the Spirit of Christ living in them do not belong to him at all.)* (Romans 8:9 NLT).

Humans are spirit beings. God gave us a soul and a body. Before our salvation, our spirit was dead, which means that only our soul and body were functioning to their full potential.

Lust—Good and Bad

Our human spirit lusts with the flesh. But our new spirit hungers for Jesus. That's why the Bible tells us to not walk in the lust of the flesh—we are to walk in the Spirit. Paul tells us:

> *So I say, walk by the Spirit, and you will not gratify the desires of the flesh. For the flesh desires what is contrary to the Spirit, and the Spirit what is contrary to the flesh. They are in conflict with each other, so that you are not to do whatever you want* (Galatians 5:16-17 NIV).

Our flesh will always want the world, while the Spirit will always want the Kingdom of God. This is why the Bible does not tell us to manage our flesh. It lets us know that the flesh needs to die: *"For if you live according to the flesh, you will die; but if by the Spirit you put to death the misdeeds of the body, you will live"* (Romans 8:13 NIV).

As we seek the presence of Jesus, the hunger and thirst already in our spirit is accessed.

Remember, Jesus told Peter, James, and John: *"Watch and pray so that you will not fall into temptation. The spirit is willing, but the flesh is weak"* (Matthew 26:41; Mark 14:38 NIV). Most people place emphasis on the flesh being weak and miss that Jesus was not highlighting the weakness of the flesh. He was actually acknowledging how powerful the spirit is. Your spirit is willing! Jesus was telling them that the hunger they needed to overcome and break through the weakness of their flesh is already in their spirit.

Your spirit does not desire cars, houses, money, and other earthly things. Your spirit only desires what is of the Spirit. This is why listening to preachers who do not have power in their lives and who do not carry revelation from the Spirit will never move a believer who is *alive*. Preachers who are void of the Spirit can only minister to the carnal nature within humans. God has placed His divine nature inside you. Similar to how genetics pass certain traits to people who are in that bloodline, your spirit has the very nature of the Father's Spirit.

The key to walking in that nature is not found anywhere in the flesh. As we walk in the Spirit, which is to live by the Holy Spirit's influence, the holy desires in our newborn spirit will drown out the lust of our flesh. The Bible speaks both of the lust of the flesh and the lust of the spirit. Consider how enticing and driving the lust of the flesh can be. Lust drives people to support sex trafficking through the pornography industry, and has created strong desires that lead to people rebelling against God in their marriage, families, and other destructive behavior. Lust can be a very strong emotion.

Have you ever considered that the human spirit has a constructive lust? According to Galatians 5, we can lust to become like Jesus, which can lead you into praying until you lose track of time while in His presence. The spirit's strong desire will lead you to a church that has five-hour meetings and you don't even realize that much time has passed. There is a passion in your spirit that will lead you to places where the word convicts and confronts sin in your life, sin that is hindering a deep, intimate relationship with your Father.

Filled With God's Essence

We haven't scratched the surface of how powerful our newly born spirit is. The Bible says that we are *"partakers of the divine nature"* of God in Second Peter 1:4 (KJV). The Bible also says

> *His divine power has given to us all things that pertain to life and godliness, through the knowledge of Him who called us by glory and virtue, by which have been given to us exceedingly great and precious promises, that through these you may be partakers of the divine nature, having escaped the corruption that is in the world through lust* (2 Peter 1:3-4 NKJV).

This means you and I are filled with the very essence of God. In fact, the Bible calls God, the "Father of spirits" (Hebrews 12:9 NKJV). This means God is the original Source of all spirits including the human spirit.

Many people emphasize how God breathed into Adam and he became a living soul. This was not the moment the human spirit was created—this was the moment when Adam's spirit was breathed into his human body. It's unclear how the soul was created, but we know with certainty that after God breathed into Adam, he had a spirit, soul, and body. The primary part of Adam was the spirit, and the spirit's fabric is the very breath of God.

This is why the human spirit is eternal. Think of a person who breathes their last breath. The breath they received from

God goes back to Him, because God's breath cannot die. Your spirit was made to live forever because its Source has no death in it. Your spiritual awakening is the key to walking in the supernatural. When the spirit comes to life again—born again—we instantly begin to experience dreams, visions, translations, transportations, angelic encounters, and every dimension of the supernatural that we see in Scripture and read about in history. God deals with the human spirit; the spirit is like the body of the spirit world, similar to how the physical body is the body of the natural world. So once we are born again, we actually naturally begin to experience the glory realm.

Reason, Logic, and Intellect

And we have received God's Spirit (not the world's spirit), so we can know the wonderful things God has freely given us. When we tell you these things, we do not use words that come from human wisdom. Instead, we speak words given to us by the Spirit, using the Spirit's words to explain spiritual truths. But people who aren't spiritual can't receive these truths from God's Spirit. It all sounds foolish to them and they can't understand it, for only those who are spiritual can understand what the Spirit means. Those who are spiritual can evaluate all things, but they themselves cannot be evaluated by others. For, "Who can know the Lord's thoughts? Who knows enough to teach him?" But we understand these things, for we have the mind of Christ (1 Corinthians 2:12-16)

The apostle Paul is saying that people who are not born again do not accept the things of the Spirit of God because they seem foolish. Why is that? Humans naturally only believe in what is empirically observed or proven.

Because the gospel is spiritual, the hindrance to the supernatural by many is their unrenewed mind, which has no access to the supernatural and is filled with carnality. The carnal mind rebels against the things of God's Kingdom. Also, our minds are filled with scientific teachings that we have received throughout our life.

The imagination is the operation of the spirit of our mind and is connected to the spirit world. There are no limitations in the spiritual realm or in our imagination. Yet, and unfortunately, children are taught against the imagination—to trust only what they see. There is nothing you can't imagine, because the spirit world has no limitations. Yet, from the earliest moments of our childhood we are taught to not believe in spiritual things.

Things we are taught can be true in the natural, but the natural was designed to be influenced by the spirit world. When people have no access to the supernatural, they can't align their life to Heaven. Reason and logic can only take us so far. Though we can experience some level of progress in the spirit realm, it may not be completed, because true progress and lasting change come from the realm of eternity.

The Bible speaks of this and says that *"knowledge puffs up"* (1 Corinthians 8:1 NIV), while Colossians 2:3 (NIV) clearly tells us that in God are, *"all the treasures of wisdom and knowledge."* God has to renew our minds from the natural to the spiritual for us to gain His wisdom and knowledge. The Bible says in Romans 12:2 for us not to be conformed to the world but to be transformed by the renewing of our minds. If our mind isn't renewed to agree with our Father, we are instantly confined to the limits of science.

Spiritual Knowledge and Wisdom

Many times the natural mind is why it's hard for people to flow in the supernatural, even after salvation. Any area that we don't understand concerning God's Kingdom becomes an area of blindness. This is what the Bible calls the darkness of the mind:

> *Their minds are full of darkness; they wander far from the life God gives because they have closed their minds and hardened their hearts against him* (Ephesians 4:18 NLT).

The more Jesus and His Kingdom are revealed to us, the more our minds will be renewed and our hearts softened.

It's possible to believe in the supernatural in one area while rejecting another. For example, many people believe in angels while rejecting the supernatural teaching of giving. Some believe in prophecy while rejecting deliverance. Some may enjoy a few prophetic words, but they don't think people can enter Heaven alive. All because they lack revelation in certain areas while having revelation in another.

THE MORE REVELATION WE RECEIVE, THE MORE OUR MINDS WILL BE RENEWED AND OUR HEARTS SOFTENED.

As our minds are re-renewed, we are no longer carnal in our thinking and our natural mind is able to submit to what God is placing in our spirit. Then we are in the position where our spirit can receive divine communication; and as that communication flows from our spirit to our mind, we are more able to receive it.

Many times when we first get saved, God begins a process of teaching us through discipleship. I can't overstate how much of a blessing it is to submit to someone who carries the secrets and mysteries of Heaven from their friendship with God. Real discipleship accelerates us into glory in short periods of time because we are following someone who knows the paths of the spirit and can learn them. Submitting to authentic apostolic/prophetic leadership will challenge carnality and teach us to walk in the ways of Jesus through repentance.

We can't repent what is in our thoughts if we don't realize what's there; we can only repent to the level of our knowledge. This is why the Bible says repent daily (Matthew 6:9-13). The closer we are to Jesus, the more we realize areas in us that are not like Him. The highest call is Christlikeness; because through His character as well as His power that flows through us, we become manifested and fruitful sons and daughters.

Prayer

Father,

In Jesus' name I thank You for the Spirit of adoption. I thank You for Your fatherhood. You are my Protector and my Provider and I thank You that You are not only a good Father but You are the perfect Father. I thank You for maturing me so that I can become a mature child of God and receive my divine inheritance. In Jesus' name I pray, amen.

6

REALMS OF HEALING
AND MIRACLES

It was a cold night in Columbus, Ohio. I had just met my future wife two days before. We had been talking on the phone for hours each day, and this particular night God had something special in store for us. At the beginning of our conversation, Emily began to tell me about a rare disease she had, along with rheumatoid arthritis, that was causing her a lot of pain. As she talked, I felt the Lord was telling me to pray for her. I mentioned it to her and soon we got lost in our conversation.

All I could think about was how beautiful and intelligent she was. Something was so different about her; and to be honest, I was already in love. Time flies when you're having fun, and before I knew it, it was very late, and we had already been on the phone for two days in a row. I was starting to get sleepy so I prepared to get off the phone. But then I sensed God reminding me to pray for Emily. I gently reminded her that I wanted to pray for her health issues. She said she would appreciate it.

I began to pray, and didn't get past, "Father, in Jesus' name..." when instantly I felt a strong surge of power rush through the phone. The atmosphere was filled with power. The anointing of God was at work. I could hear her crying, laughing, and screaming. Something was definitely happening. I was afraid to say the wrong thing, so I decided the safest way to stay out of God's way by praying in the Spirit. As I prayed, I continued to listen through the phone as Emily was having an encounter with God.

Three hours went by in a flash, then I could hear Emily lightly sobbing and I knew she was overwhelmed. I asked, "Do you feel any more pain?" I will never forget her reply. "No!" Her voice was full of joy!

Emily told me that she felt something like hammering start from the tip of her toes and went up to the top of her head. The arthritis had left her body. A miracle had taken place! What a holy moment! We praised God the rest of the night. That was also the night we knew God had divinely put us together. Emily's life was never the same again—and neither was mine.

You just read about my first miracle. What an honor that it was for the woman who would become my wife.

Now I want to share some of the many keys I have learned throughout the years, so you too can be ready to walk in healings and miracles.

There are six realms of miracles. Let's look at each one and the scriptural foundations for each. Then I will share some of my personal miracle insights.

Six Realms of Miracles

1. Healing Miracles
2. Notable Miracles
3. Special Miracles
4. Creative Miracles
5. Provision Miracles
6. Creation Miracles

1. Healing Miracles

Let's begin with healing miracles. As you can see from the list, miracles exceed physical healings, but there are healing miracles. To understand the dynamics, we must first understand healings as a foundation. The Bible tells us that when we lay hands on the sick, they will recover (Mark 16:18). When healings happen, it's remarkable and we should never discredit it.

Healings will often include a recovery time. An example of this are the lepers who were healed as they walked (Luke 17:12-16). Miracles are more instantaneous; but ultimately, the two are so intertwined that I label them almost in the same category. A healing is simply when someone who has a sickness or disease is delivered from that physical suffering. We need to simplify our understanding, or we will find ourselves arguing if someone received a miracle or a healing rather than rejoicing over the person's encounter with God.

Miracles are defined as the intervention of God when God adjusts natural laws. Miracles are part of the authentication of what is recorded in the Gospels (Matthew 4:23 for one of many examples throughout the Bible). Miracles also give witness to the resurrection of Jesus. They prove that Jesus Christ rose from the dead (see John 20).

It's important to note the miraculous has levels, much like the prophetic dimensions. Some standard miracles include casting out devils and recovery of the sick. Generally the lower levels of miracles are not creative, they don't involve the use of a cloth, and they can sometimes be denied by eyewitnesses, though they are extremely powerful. Some even categorize healings as a type of miracle. It's not important as long as you are not operating in a healing anointing trying to do creative miracles. I will cover secrets of the miracle realm later in the chapter.

2. Notable Miracles

Notable miracles are powerful because they are noteworthy—remarkable or worthy of being noticed. In Acts 3:1-10 (NKJV) when the lame man at the Beautiful Gate was healed, he began to leap and jump with joy. He had been lame from birth and everyone knew he couldn't walk because he would beg outside of the temple daily. After he received the miracle, he leaped up and praised God in the temple. Everyone who saw him was filled with awe. The miracle was so notable that when the Pharisees plotted to discredit it, they could not. The Bible says everyone was *"filled with wonder and amazement at what had happened to him."*

This class of miracles is remarkable because they are undeniable—there are many witnesses. Often these miracles involve people who are clearly disabled, clearly blind, etc. It's possible to witness a standard miracle, which doesn't leave you awestruck. Notable miracles cause people utter astonishment, including those who are trying to discredit your ministry. These miracles make the skeptics either hard-hearted or they will repent and glorify God.

3. *Special Miracles*

This class of miracles involves an unusual or special way God releases His miracle-working power. Examples include when God produced miracles through the handkerchiefs that had touched Paul's body. The anointing for miracles transferred from the cloth to demon-possessed people and the evil spirits were expelled (Acts 19:12 NLT). I believe we have only begun to scratch the surface of this type of miracle. God can and does use unusual methods to release miracles. Clothes, water, a staff, stones. In a sense, the smooth stone David used to kill Goliath was a special miracle, as was the jawbone of a donkey that Samson used to miraculously defeat his enemy (see 1 Samuel 17:32-50; Judges 15:15-16 NIV).

4. Creative Miracles

Creative miracles are remarkable. God recreates damaged parts of the human body, including organs, cells, nerve endings, bones, cartilage, muscles, teeth, growing hair on bald heads, and so on. Metal rods and screws that have been placed during surgery can dissolve mysteriously as God's power moves. This dimension of miracles also creates missing body parts that were never on the body or were detached, such as limbs.

Maybe you have had to have a kidney removed; you can receive a new one. There are no limits in Jesus. This is easy for God because He is the One who causes our bones to grow as we age from children to adults. He is the reason our hair and nails grow daily. His very nature is creative. The power that forms a baby in the womb is the same power that creates the umbilical cord that mysteriously connects the baby to the mother to provide nutrients. The same power that creates the sac and fills it with amniotic fluid is the same power that can create throughout our lives.

5. Miracles of Provision

Miracles of provision happen as God multiplies a necessity supernaturally or creates the provision from nothing. This miracle takes place when God causes money to appear in a random place, like the mouth of a fish: *"Nevertheless, lest we offend them, go to the sea, cast in a hook, and take the fish that comes up first. And when you have opened its mouth, you will find a piece of money; take that and give it to them for Me and you"* (Matthew 17:27 NKJV). And, of course, the well-known

Bible story of Jesus feeding more than 5,000 people with only two loaves of bread and five fish (see Matthew 14:17-21).

6. *Miracles in Creation*

Miracles in creation stem from the dominion that God gave Adam in the beginning. We were given authority over everything in the seas, on and under the earth, and the air. Because of this dominion that was given back to us through the death and resurrection of Jesus, we can operate in authority over creation for God's Kingdom purposes. This is how Elijah could call down fire, Samuel could command rain, and Elijah could stop as well as start rain to fall on earth.

Toward the end of this chapter we will cover practical ways to actually operate in each of these realms. But before that, I want to expose a missing link in many people's modern miracle and healing ministries. The mere mention of this makes some cringe. Yet I firmly believe that the ministry of healing, miracles, and deliverance are intertwined, and is proven in Scripture.

Demonstrating the Spirit's Power

Revelation Knowledge

Revelation knowledge is a major key to operating in healings and miracles. Revelation is knowledge and secrets that God reveals pertaining to something in the spirit realm. It is not logical, intellectual, or rooted in reason. Because this type of knowledge is divine, it is of the spirit world, which operates higher than natural understanding. Scripture tells us that God framed the worlds (in plural form). This refers to the spiritual world and the natural world.

The spiritual world is far superior than the natural world; and therefore, knowledge associated with that world is superior. The spiritual world is not limited by laws that govern our physical world. Revelation reveals secrets and mysteries in the Kingdom. In relation to demonstrating the power of God, the revelation may be a particular way God leads you to pray for a person; or the revelation may be a pattern on how to heal a certain sickness or disease.

Examples include the following so you can have a clear understanding of what I mean.

Revelation that comes to you for a specific person's healing will involve the Lord's voice. He will communicate with your spiritual senses, your heart, or your mind with a subtle suggestion or leading. You may dream the night before and see exactly how to heal the person. Or a mental picture or image may flash in your mind while you're praying for the person. Maybe a sudden thought pops into your mind that you need to tell the person. Maybe you sense the name of the sickness, or feel led to lay hands in a certain place or a certain way. God may even tell you to have the person stand in a certain spot. This does not cover all the ways God may voice His instructions, but are good examples of how revelation of sickness can be revealed. When we follow the lead of the Spirit, explosive miracles and healings happen.

These leadings can become patterns that God reveals often to you. You will recognize when a pattern develops and if you apply that reality, it will work in similar situations. In the case of miracles and healings, He may show you how to pray for a sickness and then following that pattern will work every time. This is not the same as a method. A method is when we create something based on natural knowledge.

A divine pattern is given to us based on how the spirit realm works; therefore, it is not just for one situation. It can produce positive results again and again. A pattern that the Lord has given me with cancer is to curse death and infirmity. This means I don't have to wait for revelation to pray for the sick. I follow the original command of Jesus and pray for the person; but along the way, I gain knowledge on how to become more effective and patterns are revealed that can be applied again and again—unless otherwise directed by the Holy Spirit.

A woman who had stage-four ovarian cancer attended one of our ministry meetings. After I finished preaching, I was made aware that they had driven three hours to get to our service and they explained her health situation to me. I cursed cancer, death, and infirmity, and commanded the disease to come out of her. She shook as the power of God went through her. Two weeks later it was medically verified that she was cancer-free.

We have seen many people healed of cancer. This happens because I understand and have wisdom for how to apply a revelation from God.

The following is a list to help you as a foundation when you pray for sickness and disease to be healed.

- Infirmity spirit. Causes strange illnesses, diseases that confound doctors and can't be diagnosed, and sicknesses/diseases caused by demons.

- Deaf spirit. Causes people to be deaf with speech difficulties.

- Lunatic spirit. Causes mental illnesses.

- Blindness spirit. Unable to see.

- All sickness and disease are connected to death and the grave. I almost always curse these things when I pray for the sick.

Different Administrations of Healing

There are several ways healings and miracles can be administered.

- You can operate in them by faith, which is to simply believe God's Word and lay hands on people. Pray because you know God heals, understand His covenant, and trust that His Word is true. You can use oil for this prayer.

- You can operate in healing by the gifts of the Spirit. The gift of faith will cluster with healings and miracles. The gifts often activate when you are doing Kingdom work.

- You can operate in healing by healing atmospheres. The atmospheres of faith, anointing, and glory enhance the gifts and we see greater results as we enter each realm. When we enter the glory and it increases and becomes greater, we will see more angelic activity and the miraculous.

Casting Out Demons

One of the major ways to see an increase in healing and miracles is to begin to engage in spiritual warfare and deliverance. Many of the sicknesses and diseases that were healed by Jesus were rooted in the demonic. In Scripture the healing and deliverance ministry are closely intertwined with one another. Jesus cast out demons. We can't say we want to do His work and ignore this particular ministry. To ignore deliverance ministry would mean to leave many sick and oppressed with the devil, all while telling them how much God loves them. One of the ministries we were anointed for is to open the doors of captives—to set prisoners free.

There are no particular "deliverance" ministries. All ministries should deliver people who are in bondage. Deliverance is one of the signs that follow the believer, every believer—not only apostles, prophets, evangelists, pastors, and teachers. All of us can learn to operate in this ministry. A.A. Allen, known for explosive and remarkable miracles, declared, "You foul demon of cancer, leave this body!" and people would be raised up from their deathbed. About Smith Wigglesworth, people stated, "He doesn't punch people, he punches devils, but people just get in the way."

I can't cover deliverance in detail; however, I want to give you some tips for casting out demons based on a divine pattern that God has given me. Whenever I begin to do deliverance, I understand that in every case it is not as simple as just telling the demon to come out. I first begin with walking the person or the corporate group through repentance. In my experience, I have discovered several primary hindrances to deliverance. The first is *evil covenants*. In the spiritual realm, covenants are very powerful. We see God answer the cries of the people being oppressed by Egypt because of the covenant that He made with Abraham, Isaac, and Jacob.

Today we are saved within the New Covenant. A covenant in a general sense is an agreement between two parties. Covenants affect generations. Evil covenants do the same, but bind a person and their generations to satan's kingdom. For this reason, I always begin by leading the person through repentance and to renounce every evil covenant in their generations. I then proceed through the same process for generational curses, all sin, and iniquity—sins that are passed from generation to generation. Remember that repentance is for our entire bloodline as well as what we ourselves have done.

Spiritual Warfare

After we have stripped away every legal right of the kingdom of darkness in our lives through repentance and the cleansing power of the blood of Jesus makes all things new, I do spiritual warfare prayer and command demons to come out by the fire of the Holy Spirit, the anointing, the blood of Jesus, and other spiritual weapons. During spiritual warfare, demons go running, including spirits that cause diseases, death, paralysis, cancer, aids, HIV, and more. I have spoken directly to cancer and watched it leave people's bodies. I have seen MS leave people, and I have watched spirits that caused deafness leave people's ears.

In a service in Maryland, I was preaching on why the church must have the power of God. A woman was brought to the service who had two oxygen tanks. One was pushed by her daughter. She had been on oxygen for months due to stage-four lung cancer. She worked her way to the altar as I was praying for the sick, and her daughter told me her story. I laid hands on the woman and commanded cancer, death, and infirmity to come out of her.

She left that day without needing oxygen. Her oxygen levels were perfectly normal after receiving healing by the power of Jesus. Not all illnesses are caused by demons, but many of them certainly are. We must rely on the Holy Spirit's voice and discerning of spirits to know when certain prayers are needed. Remember, being used by God has everything to do with being led by the Spirit.

The Glory Realm of Healing and Miracles

When the glory of God is in operation, none of these normal steps are necessary. Everything mentioned in this chapter must be understood in relation to the anointing. The glory is Heaven's atmosphere, and within Heaven everything that operates within the law of sin and death can't live in the glory—in the glory there is only the law of the Spirit of life. Sickness, disease, and death are incinerated when the realms of glory are being experienced. So when the glory comes, all we must do is stand in the glory. Simply get out of the way and encourage the people that everything that they need is available.

Lord, manifest Your glory right now.

Fresh Infilling, Fire, and Power

Having a fresh baptism of the Holy Spirit is a key to moving in the power of God. We need a baptism right now. The Bible says that Stephen was full of faith and power (Acts 6:5 NIV). I always know when I am going to see the greatest demonstrations of God's power in my life—when I am full from spending time with Jesus. I can feel the weight of what's in my spirit. There is nothing like being saturated in His presence. The more you are full of His presence, the more power, fire, and faith will be inside you.

This is why Jesus was teaching the disciples about fasting in order to cast out doubt and unbelief. When we spend time with Jesus in the Spirit, His word becomes real to us and a faith enters our heart to see it. The more we seek Him, the more real He becomes. Although the Holy Spirit's power and fire are not constant, His presence is. It's not that we lose the Holy Spirit's presence; what decreases is the power and the fire.

This is why Peter said it was not good for the apostles to wait on tables and how they needed to give themselves *"continually to prayer and to the ministry of the word"* (Acts 6:4 NKJV). Anyone who will be used by God in the supernatural must embrace continually ministering to God in prayer, fasting, and His word. Peter recognized that he needed to receive fresh impartation to keep advancing the Kingdom with power.

The very first time I ever preached was when the pastor asked me the day before if I could preach. With such short notice and because it was my first time, I was very nervous. That night I stayed up the entire night to prepare for the meeting, praying and trying to figure out what I should do or say. Then I lay down on my face and just worshipped. Eventually there were no more words.

One of the greatest keys to prayer can be found in Psalm 80:18 (NLT): *"Then we will never abandon you again. Revive us so we can call on your name once more."* A major key to effective prayer is to enter His presence and stay there. As He revived me, tears began to flow. I never went back to saying words, but as I was weeping He filled me with His power. I'm not sure how many hours it was, but I cried until I eventually fell asleep.

When I ministered the following day I was full of power. I was extra sensitive to the voice and leadings of the Spirit, and the glory of God manifested. My words had authority. The things I spoke were weighty and full of life. The words of God through me seemed to baptize the people like in Acts 10:44 (NLT): *"Even as Peter was saying these things, the Holy Spirit fell upon all who were listening to the message."*

"YOU WILL PREACH IN THE REALM THAT YOU PRAY IN."

The church where I was giving the message was "religious." Nevertheless, I felt fire fall from Heaven into the room.

People were in awe and wonder as they experienced the glory fire of God—many for the first time. People had encounters with God and came out of religion. I will never forget what God spoke to me about preaching. He told me that night while I was on the floor, "You will preach in the realm that you pray in."

From that day on, I learned to prioritize, not prepare a message. I prepare my spirit by positioning myself to receive a fresh infilling. What's more amazing is that you don't have to be scheduled to preach to experience this! You can simply be a lover of Jesus and want to be full. Embrace this lifestyle and you will see God's power flow through you. The power is not in a baptism that you received years ago—it's in every fresh encounter.

Impartation

Impartation of the Spirit is one way we can walk in the power of God in a greater way. Impartation can instantly download gifts of the Spirit, graces, and even authority for ministry promotion. Impartation is a divine transfer of power. We can receive an impartation from an encounter with Jesus, or an angel. Typically people who go on to have powerful ministries can trace the power in their ministry to an encounter with God.

As mentioned earlier in the book, Moses' encounter with God through a burning bush filled him with God's wonders. The key to this type of impartation is to chase after God with all of your heart. If you don't encounter Him, add a day. Tell yourself that you are not going to stop until you encounter

Him. One moment in His glory can change you and empower you for the rest of your life.

Sometimes impartation can even be God releasing strength to you in hard times. An example of this is when the angel came to Jesus to give Him strength to endure the imminent process of dying on the cross (see Luke 22:42-44). I have experienced this as well. In a hard time I woke up in the middle of the night and was surrounded by angels. There was a golden glow around me and I received strength that helped me during that hard time.

I have also received impartation in dreams. I received the gift of prophecy in a dream where I saw an apostle come and prophesy over me about the gift. I woke up shaking; and from that moment on, I could prophesy. I also received the working of miracles through impartation in a dream. In the dream the voice of the Lord spoke through a prophet whom I highly respected. The Voice said, "Miracles are in your hands!" I woke up and my hands were burning with fire. Not long after this, miracles occurred.

Impartation can also come through ministers who carry what we need. If a person carries a gift of the Spirit, they can impart that gift to others. The same is true of the anointing grace. Impartation can be released through the laying on of hands and prophecy. This is what Paul meant when he says in Second Timothy 1:6 (NKJV), *"stir up the gift of God which is in you through the laying on of my hands."* The Lord will lead you to the right leadership and use them to impart into you. He will also send apostles and prophets to come and speak into your life who may impart into you. We can receive impartation from listening to YouTube videos, podcasts, and virtually anything God's power can be transferred through.

Miracles Follow

A very practical truth is that miracles will not follow a person who does not *go* with the gospel, sharing the Good News. It's important to put yourself in the position to be used by God. I encourage you to preach faith! Preach miracles! Preach signs and wonders! Declare God's power over the power of the devil and move out in faith.

Prayer

Holy Spirit,

We ask You to fill the atmosphere right now. I ask You to use me the way You used the people in Scripture. Work with me to do miracles in the way that You used Jesus. Flow through my life so I may do greater works. Right now, I ask to heal the sick, raise the dead, open blind eyes, see the lame walk, and do creative miracles.

Today I reveal mindsets in my life that hinder and restrict the power of God. Right now, let the fire of the Holy Spirit roast every anti-supernatural spirit that would try to frustrate my miracle ministry. Right now, baptize me in the Spirit of might and counsel, in Jesus' name. Fill me with faith and power. I thank You for allowing me to do so many miracles and healings that I lose count. In Jesus' name, amen.

7

SUPERNATURAL WISDOM AND REVELATION

That the God of our Lord Jesus Christ,
the Father of glory, may give to you the
spirit of wisdom and revelation in the
knowledge of Him (Ephesians 1:17 NKJV).

Wisdom and revelation go hand and hand. It is impossible to operate in the supernatural without both.

Spirit of Wisdom

I want to begin with the spirit of wisdom—wisdom is a spirit. The Bible says that wisdom assisted in the creation of everything in the beginning. This means wisdom played a role in the creation of the visible *and* invisible worlds with all their intrinsic operating functions. Wisdom was involved in the very detail of the cosmos, which means the order (systematic functionality) and arrangement (placement) of all creation. This is critical to understand to avoid underrating wisdom.

Wisdom is powerful because wisdom is a key that unlocks the secret of how things work in the Spirit. Once we understand how the realm of the Spirit works, we can access the realities experientially. This is why many people who are not necessarily prophetic still seem to live holistic lives. They have gained wisdom from the Bible about finances, stewardship, marriage, and so on.

I know many prophetic people whose lives are in ruins because they have revelation with no wisdom. They can see something in their spirit but have no idea how to retrieve it. This causes the prophetic to seem like it is no better than a fairy-tale book being read at nap time. The lack of wisdom among immature prophetic people has essentially caused the prophetic to be rejected.

I often joke with my friends about what I call "looney tune ministry." I have heard prophetic words about food that you would put on a grill dancing behind me as I preach and all kinds of things. Sometimes it's immaturity; very often it is that the supernatural is not taught concisely. The root is a lack of wisdom about how spiritual activities truly work. One of my biggest concerns is not just the demonic or immaturity, it's also mental illness.

Mental Illness

Someone can be filled with the Spirit and have the anointing while at the same time be mentally ill. In fact to some degree, mental illness can hide within a supernatural culture because many churches don't do well enough when biblically unpacking what the supernatural actually is. When we fail to articulate the authentic supernatural, the lack of definition leaves room for error, witchcraft, vain imaginations posing as visions, and last but not least, mental illness posing as spirituality.

Therefore, it is extremely important not to water down the supernatural realm to the point where everything is considered an act of God. Bubbles in a bathtub are usually not speaking. I often see this epidemic on seer Facebook groups, etc. Some is ignorance, some immaturity, and some consist of people who need professional help. The bottom line is that diluting the spiritually supernatural world creates enabling mental illness environments.

This is a real issue, and one that I am becoming more and more concerned about as I watch the charismatic movement. I believe God is raising up people like the apostle Paul who so clearly expounded on all spiritual matters including gifts of the Spirit. We must clearly define language and make distinctions about the spiritual so we can distinguish the authentic supernatural from everything else. This will better position us to help both those who may have mental illness and those who need to mature in the spiritual realm.

IT'S NOT ENOUGH TO BE REVELATORY, WE MUST BECOME PEOPLE OF WISDOM.

I have heard of people doing the craziest things, all in the name of the prophetic. Some have caused damage to themselves and many others. It's not enough to be revelatory, we must become people of wisdom. Usually as we grow and mature spiritually, we can look back and laugh at what we claimed God told us to do. I have avoided telling you about silliness in my immaturity, but now I share the following funny story with you…just don't judge me (wink).

Years ago I felt like God told me to dress like I held the highest position in my work field. Sounds good right? Well, not if you overdressed. The highest people in my work environment wore polo shirts and I wore a three-piece suit. I even walked with a briefcase filled with nothing. I was convinced that I was walking out a prophetic word involving Jacob wearing the goat hair to get the blessing from Isaac.

Well, after a year and a half I was fired. Apparently I missed God. It wasn't funny to me at the time, but looking back it is. When we are just beginning to learn how to process revelation, we will often miss it. Trust the leadership that God has given you. A great way to grow in wisdom is listening to those who have gone before you. This will save you from having to share embarrassing stories like this one of mine. Wisdom is an important part of moving in God's supernatural power.

Filled With Wisdom

And when the Sabbath had come, He [Jesus] *began to teach in the synagogue. And many hearing Him were astonished, saying, "Where did this Man get these things? And what wisdom is this which is given to Him, that such mighty works are performed by His hands!* (Mark 6:2 NKJV)

As we discuss the Scripture from Mark 6:2, it's clear that the Jewish people believed the mighty works Jesus did were the result of wisdom. We don't often think of wisdom in relation to moving in power, but it's important to realize that the more you understand the glory of God, the more you will experience it. This is why Habakkuk 2:14 (NIV) tells us, *"For the earth will be filled with the knowledge of the glory of the Lord as the waters cover the sea."* As the knowledge of the glory increases, the more we will know how to move and operate within it.

For example, it's possible to be in a prophetic environment and not know how to prophesy. While having drastic encounters with the Lord, I joined a prophetic school at age nineteen. I halfheartedly did the homework, which was packed with wisdom. At the end of the course I couldn't prophesy. The issue was not that I was not prophetic. The issue was that I had no wisdom concerning operating in the prophetic to edify, comfort, and exhort. The same can be applied to deliverance, miracles, healings, raising the dead, and so on.

WISDOM PROVIDES THE SECRETS TO RELEASING THE KINGDOM ON EARTH.

Wisdom provides the secrets to releasing the Kingdom on earth. The "how to" releases demonstrations of the Spirit. The possibilities of what wisdom can obtain in the Spirit are endless. Wisdom can guide us to wealth and more. The best way to communicate this is that the depths of wisdom give you the potential to experience the full spectrum of the supernatural. Whatever area you gain wisdom in, you will see more of that aspect of the Kingdom in your life.

Revelation and Wisdom

That the God of our Lord Jesus Christ, the Father of glory, may give to you the spirit of wisdom and revelation in the knowledge of Him, the eyes of your understanding being enlightened; that you may know what is the hope of His calling, and what the riches of the glory of His inheritance in the saints (Ephesians 1:17-18 NKJV).

Now let's talk about revelation. As stated earlier, wisdom and revelation go hand and hand. To have your eyes of understanding enlightened, both are required. Revelation is when something in the invisible word is made known to us by the spirit—when the unknown becomes known. The issue the religious leaders had was that they had no revelation. They simply memorized the Scriptures. This is why Jesus was among them fulfilling the signs that He was the Messiah—yet His identity was still unknown to them.

The Pharisees wanted the move of God. They studied the law and the prophets so well that they could say the prophecies and the law verbatim. When Jesus came in the flesh they resisted Him because they had no revelation of God. They had their own interpretation of what God should be, so much so that they developed a stronghold that blinded them from receiving the glory manifesting right in front of them.

It's very important that we have more than head knowledge. The religious leaders actually witnessed Jesus' life and yet were unchanged. The difference between those who move with God and those who resist and oppose what He is doing is a lack of recognizing and accepting God's revelation.

We can only know God through revelation. Without revelation we are blind. This is why Jesus referred to the religious leaders of His day as the blind leading the blind (see Matthew 15:14). Also, Ephesians 1:18 tells us that through revelation we can know *the hope of His calling* and the *inheritance* inside us. We will never tap into all that is inside us until we have the Spirit of revelation. Far too many Christians have no idea what's inside, thus we appear powerless because of ignorance.

God has certainly not run out of power! We simply don't know our inheritance after the church stopped teaching the full apostolic doctrine that the apostles learned from Jesus in the flesh when He was in His glorified body forty days and forty nights after His resurrection. This is the equivalent of when Moses was on the mountain of God for forty days and nights. Moses received the Old Covenant and the apostles were taught what they needed to know about the New Covenant pertaining to the Kingdom. It is time we learn about and accept our inheritance.

Divine Knowledge

The point I'm making is that they could not study and receive divine knowledge. Divine knowledge is revealed through revelation. With the completion of the Bible, nothing we receive will add or take away from the Bible. All authentic revelation aligns with the Holy Scriptures and the character and nature of Jesus. This is not to be mistaken with the belief that Scriptures are to be taken verbatim. For example, if you have a dream and God shows you the name of your new job, there will be no Scripture to validate this dream as authentic. Authentic revelation will not necessarily be specific Scriptures—but at the same time, authentic revelation will never alter or diminish Scripture. Always remember that anything that changes or even diminishes who Jesus is, is demonic in nature and must be rejected.

Several years ago I was teaching a revelatory word on spiritual warfare. A man who was visiting our church in Jacksonville, Florida, told me after service that he learned more in two hours than he had in the past ten years of attending church. While I am thankful for God giving me the Spirit of wisdom and revelation, I was also saddened by this. It reminded me of the lack of fresh manna that some experience, though they faithfully attend church. Every Christian should be receiving fresh manna—fresh meat of the Word of God that sustains and strengthens us.

Revelation Is…

Revelation is very important because it breaks off the seals of the Word and opens us to the secrets and mysteries of the Bible. Revelation is also what moves spiritual things into the natural realm to be manifested and experienced. There is much resistance in the spiritual realm to hinder revelation from reaching the earth. This is why we need the revelation ministries of the apostles and prophets to marry intercession.

We often don't consider that the prince of Persia was trying to hinder the angelic messenger from bringing revelation to Daniel while he was praying for understanding of his dream (see Daniel 10). Did you catch that? The war was about stopping a dream interpretation. Hell knows that if revelation reaches the prophets and a prophetic people, manifestation will happen on earth.

Revelation is also the sword of the Lord. God-breathed revelation is the sword of the Spirit according to Ephesians 6:17. The sword of the Spirit is the word of God, the *rhema* of God. Revelation is a powerful weapon, and is why Paul told Timothy that with his prophecies he could fight a good battle. Without prophecies we are not properly equipped for warfare.

> *Timothy, my son, I am giving you this command in keeping with the prophecies once made about you, so that by recalling them you may fight the battle well, holding on to faith and a good conscience, which some have rejected and so have suffered shipwreck with regard to the faith* (1 Timothy 1:18-19 NIV).

We need revelation. We need prophetic leadership. We need prophetic houses and believers with prophetic DNA. We need pioneers, forerunners, and reformers. All of these types of people emerge as fresh revelation is released to the church.

These roles birthed by revelation covering the earth, are a major threat to the enemy. They press into dimensions of God that have either been neglected since a previous generation accessed it or even since ancient times, causing them to be new to this generation.

Pioneers discover Heaven's secrets and mysteries that upgrade the body of believers. These supernatural upgrades build us up corporately over time into the full stature of Christ. When you are a forerunner, the impact and fruit of your life is hard to measure. People who lack prophetic foresight will miss how remarkable the infant stages of what you are doing is by comparing it to what already exists.

FORERUNNERS ARE CALLED TO HAVE A GREATER IMPACT ON THE FUTURE THAN THE PRESENT.

You may be mocked and people may be waiting to see you fail. You test the narrow-minded and offend people who are stuck in their ways. People will misunderstand you and walk away from you because they are looking for an already established road. But you are called to uncharted territories. There is no terminology for you yet, but know this—in the future, a generation will glean from what you do now. A forerunner is called to have a greater impact on the future than the present.

Revelation is vast and can cover many areas within the supernatural. Anything can be uncovered and disclosed to us for Kingdom purposes. A simple key to growing in both wisdom and revelation is to have a healthy biblical foundation. Having the Bible within you gives the Holy Spirit the opportunity to uncover for you the mysteries in the Scriptures. As we study diligently the Holy Spirit teaches us revelation and opens godly wisdom. I often have revelations pour out of me as I teach basic truths. Sound biblical truth provides the launching pad for God to thrust us into dimensions of revelatory articulation.

Often as we enter certain atmospheres, it's a sign that we have relocated or gained access into a new spiritual place. That place may be invisible to some, but the heavenly atmosphere can be felt in the spirit. Entering causes your spiritual senses to discern what's happening in that godly place, and Scriptures start flowing into your thoughts. I have found that the deeper I enter into the glory, the more my spirit gains knowledge, even just from the atmosphere. Whenever any of the five spiritual senses become active, we must learn to tune into what God wants us to discern.

If you think your brain has incredible storage, consider the capacity of your spirit to archive Scriptures and the words God has spoken. Often these are filed away until the appointed time for revelation comes. For me, this happens as I preach. I don't try to go into revelation—I'm often overtaken by the divine flow and utterance of the Spirit of revelation to empower people and advance them in the ways of God.

Revelation is a door. You can enter what has been revealed to you by faith. Wherever you have revelation from the Holy Spirit, you have authority.

Also keep in mind there are hindrances to gaining revelation. The enemy doesn't want us to have revelation because he doesn't want us to access the supernatural or to have faith in God. The enemy knows that faith is directly linked to revelation, so he hinders us from perceiving spiritual things.

The enemy hinders us from experiencing God in the supernatural with spiritual blindness and deafness in several ways. One way is when he places a veil over us, preventing us from seeing the glory of God. Paul tells us what we will experience after the evil veil is removed from our face. We will begin to see the manifested glory and see ourselves transformed into His image:

> But we all, with unveiled face, beholding as in a mirror the glory of the Lord, are being transformed into the same image from glory to glory, just as by the Spirit of the Lord (2 Corinthians 3:18 NKJV).

Prayer

Pray this prayer with me: In the name of Jesus, I thank You for Your blood. And right now, I repent for my generations and any sin that I have personally committed that is causing spiritual blindness or deafness in my life. I thank You that by the fire of God, every evil veil is destroyed, in Jesus' name. Amen.

8

WALKING IN THE SPIRIT

I say then: Walk in the Spirit, and you shall not
fulfill the lust of the flesh (Galatians 5:16 NKJV).

There is a distinct difference between the Spirit being *in* me, the Spirit being *on* me, and the Spirit being *with* me. Each of these dimensions make up what it means to be "baptized in the Spirit." Baptism is not only to have an infilling of the Holy Spirit. It means to be submerged in the Spirit in all of these aspects—in, on, and with. I became aware of this truth in a greater way when God began to use me.

I was part of my church's intercession team and I often experienced various dimensions of the operations and baptisms of the Spirit while leading corporate prayer. I would feel different manifestations of the Holy Spirit. Sometimes it would be tangible fire, other times I felt electricity surging through my body or a heaviness as I prayed. When this happened I became aware that much more power flowed through me than when I didn't feel Him. To this day when this happens there is a dramatic increase in the demonstration of the Spirit's power. Even as you read this, the Spirit is on you and activating you.

One example of this occurred at a conference in Harrisburg, Pennsylvania. As I was preparing to minister, I felt the glory of God—but it was different. Rather than just feeling the glory in the atmosphere, it enveloped my entire body as a garment. When I preached, the prophetic words I spoke were weighty and full of authority. Many people fell out as I was prophesying over them. Healings and miracles began to explode on people throughout the room. I believe every person I prayed for at that gathering was healed. This supernatural upgrade doesn't happen outside of God's glory.

I struggled to stay standing, so two men steadied me so I could continue to minister in the supernatural glory. The power and glory was so intense that I was being electrocuted, and so were the men helping me. There was so much going on in the room at one time that it was clear that though I was praying for people, Heaven had come rushing in.

After processing this gathering afterward, I knew that the revival glory we saw began with the Spirit coming on me as

I was preparing. I understand through experience what Oral Roberts meant when he said he would not leave the tent until he felt the Spirit or the presence on him.

Spiritual Upgrade Keys

So Jesus said to them again, "Peace to you! As the Father has sent Me, I also send you." And when He had said this, He breathed on them, and said to them, "Receive the Holy Spirit" (John 20:21-22 NKJV).

I want to share two keys that I believe will thrust you into an upgrade in doing the works of Jesus. Take note.

1. The first thing we must recognize is that the infilling of the Spirit is in the phase of baptism. As you read in John 20:22 (NIV), Jesus breathed on the disciples and said, *"Receive the Holy Spirit."* When this happened, they were infilled with His presence. Many people downplay this moment in John 20:22, but can you imagine Jesus breathing on you after being resurrected from the dead? I can't even imagine how powerful His breath was going into them. Now with that in mind, let's consider that they were still not *submerged* in the Spirit, they were only *filled.* They had presence but not power.

The Bible tells us that presence and power are not exactly the same. Acts 10:38 tells us that God anointed Jesus with *"the Holy Spirit and power."* One is the Person, and the other is power. When Jesus breathed on the disciples, they received the Person but they still needed the power.

2. In Acts 2:2-4 we read very powerful descriptions about the birth of the New Testament church. As the disciples were waiting in the upper room, the supernatural wind of God

began to rush through, creating a loud sound. Next it says fire filled the house (atmosphere).

Many times, for us to receive something from God, as it comes from the supernatural world, it arrives in an invisible form within the atmosphere. Glory atmospheres provide the substance for what is invisible to be created. We will go into more detail about this when we discuss supernatural atmospheres later in this book. The fire of God first filled the house and then came on each one of them. After that they were filled and began to speak in other tongues.

In Acts 2, the disciples were accelerated into the fullness of God. The Spirit came on them, filled them, and He was with them. We can see the evidence of Him being with them because no one invited the thousands that came that day. That was the Spirit working with them. They were fully submerged in God's fiery baptism. We are filled with the Spirit for personal transformation; we are empowered for world transformation: *"But you will receive power when the Holy Spirit comes on you; and you will be my witnesses in Jerusalem, and all Judea and Samaria, and to the ends of the earth"* (Acts 1:8 NIV).

Because there are three distinct dimensions of the Spirit being *in* you, the Spirit being *on* you, and the Spirit being *with* you, and that being "baptized in the Spirit" means to be submerged in the Spirit in all three of these aspects—let's now closely examine each dimension.

The Spirit in You

The Spirit *in* you enables you to:

- Speak with unknown tongues
- Access the anointing that teaches you mysteries and secrets tailored to your purpose
- Enjoy a prayer life without limits
- Access the prophetic anointing
- Awaken your spiritual senses and Spirit
- Fulfill the potential for each gift of the Spirit
- Understand spiritual activity
- Stir up supernatural power

I am sure you can add to this list; this is not an exhaustive list. I believe each of these points can serve as foundations to what it means to have the Holy Spirit in you. Many books have been written about speaking in tongues, so I don't go into detail in this book. But I do want to point out that receiving tongues is not enough. We must spend time using the divine languages that our spirits have been enabled to speak in order to actually see results.

People who receive the infilling but do not speak in tongues daily will live an ordinary Christian life. Being able to speak in tongues is not speaking in tongues. The supernatural realm functions by words. Words are one of the primary ways to operate in the Spirit. Your words are spiritual; this is why when people received the Holy Spirit in the book of Acts, it led to them speaking in tongues. Imagine living in a nation without being able to communicate. We will never be able to fully explain the mystery of speaking in tongues—but when we do it, we will see results.

Walk in the Spirit

This chapter is titled "Walking in the Spirit," which the Bible tells us to do in Galatians 5:16 (NKJV): *"I say then: Walk in the Spirit, and you shall not fulfill the lust of the flesh."*

Walking in the Spirit is not only to prophesy and to move in demonstrations of the Spirit, it is also to live under the influence of the Spirit. In our day-to-day life, the Lord is calling us into a lifestyle of the supernatural.

The Bible says that Jesus breathed on the disciples and instantly they received the Holy Spirit. Then Jesus instructs them to *wait* for the promise of the Father and they would be endued with power from on high (Acts 1:8). Right there are two different dimensions of walking in the Spirit. The first is when the Holy Spirit comes inside them, then they had to wait for the power—revealing to us that the infilling of the Holy Spirit does not bring the same result as the Holy Spirit being *on* us.

The Holy Spirit being *in* us brings about what Jesus speaks of in the book of John. Then Jesus describes the Holy Spirit as a comforter, teacher, and the one who will lead us and guide us into all truth—which is personal revelation and transformation.

> *And I will ask the Father, and he will give you another Advocate* [Comforter], *who will never leave you. He is the Holy Spirit, who leads into all truth. The world cannot receive him, because it isn't looking for him and doesn't recognize him. But you know him, because he lives with you now and later will be in you* (John 14:16-17 (NLT).

The Holy Spirit helps us hear the voice of the Father. The Bible also says that we don't need anyone to teach us—the anointing that dwells inside us will teach us all things (see 1 John 2:27 NKJV). When the Holy Spirit fills us, He begins to teach us all things. This means that the Holy Spirit inside us teaches us what we need to know.

When I was eighteen years old, after my salvation I began to develop a relationship with the Holy Spirit. At the time I didn't recognize that He was teaching me, but I specifically remember Him actually teaching me. It wasn't in the English language or in actual words, it was in His guidance. The Bible doesn't say that the Holy Spirit will simply teach us the truth, it says that He will guide us into all truth. The Lord wants to guide you into the truths of the spiritual realm; He wants them to be experienced. Many times when the Holy Spirit is teaching us, He's actually guiding us by the voice of God into what the Lord wants us to know. Whenever the Spirit of God is guiding you, it's a sign that He is leading you into what He wants you to experience in your life.

It's important to know that many people are filled with the Holy Spirit. Yet, because they don't spend time with God to develop a friendship with Him, they don't experience the guidance of the Holy Spirit into all truth. If I was to define religion in this context, it would be "Christianity without the supernatural." It would be people attempting to do spiritual things without the Holy Spirit and without understanding how to walk in the Spirit.

There is a story about when John G. Lake had an opportunity to meet William Seymour, who was used by God to open the realms of revival in the early 1900s in the Azusa Street Revival in Los Angeles, California. John G. Lake said that William Seymour carried more of the presence of God than anyone he had ever met. When John G. Lake met him, the presence of God was all over William Seymour.

Seymour loved the presence of God and would spend so much time with God that as he was in the Lord's presence he had an electricity about him. When Seymour would lay down on his bed with his wife, she would be electrocuted by the presence of God on him. It happened so often that she had to get up from the bed because she couldn't bear the electric presence of God that rested on Seymour.

Can you imagine carrying God's presence in that way? Many people only emphasize speaking in tongues during the Azusa Street Revival, but there were many miracles that took place at the Azusa Street mission. There were reports of people seeing actual flames shooting out from the top of the building. Fire trucks would show up and there would be no fire—the people were actually seeing the flames in the Spirit. After that, the number of miracles increased and people saw limbs growing back, bones cracking and popping, and all types of miracles and creative miracles taking place.

One of my favorite preachers in history is a woman named Maria Woodworth-Etter. She carried such a presence of God that when she entered cities, it is rumored that sometimes up to one hundred miles around the city would be affected by the prophetic glory. People would fall into trances and have encounters with Jesus. Many people were saved through these experiences. What some call trance-evangelism was the supernatural realm of the prophetic opening up and people were having dreams, visions, and translations.

I believe all this is possible and more, by becoming lovers of the presence of Jesus. We can't get there without first developing intimacy with the Holy Spirit and becoming a friend of God.

The Spirit on You

The next dimension is the Holy Spirit *on* you. Even when the Bible talks about Joel's prophecy, this dimension is described as the Spirit of God being poured out upon all flesh (Acts 2:17-21). I believe that the phrase in the King James Version *"all flesh"* is used in the Old Testament as many people did not experience the Spirit coming on them because the anointing was for prophets, priests, and kings. Temporarily included in this was the office of the judge. In the Old Testament these were the only people who carried the anointing in a continual way. Under the New Covenant, the Holy Spirit and the anointing are available to all people. When the Holy Spirit was on people in the Old Testament, there were heightened levels of the supernatural manifested.

Following are a few examples:

"The Spirit of the Lord came powerfully upon David" after he was anointed by Samuel (1 Samuel 16:13 NLT). This power led to David killing a bear and a lion with his bare hands. It also led David to slay a menacing giant at the age of thirteen. The anointing so empowered David that he could pick up the sword of Goliath and cut off his head. It's easy to read over

this, but when examined closely, the Bible was describing how large Goliath's body armor was. We can only assume that his sword was very large as well. Yet young David could pick up the sword of a giant, this was a supernatural feat!

When the Spirit of God was on Samson, he became a one-man wrecking crew. All by himself Samson could have destroyed the entire Philistine army, and they knew this. This is why they hired Delilah to seduce and trick Samson. The truth is, people who walk in this dimension of the Holy Spirit must guard themselves from the spirit of Delilah and the enemy coming up with crafty ways to cause us to self-destruct. When the enemy knows that he can't defeat you head-on, he will find creative ways to strategically counter maneuver to weaken your anointing.

After Elijah prophesied to King Ahab about a drought. *"The power of the Lord came on Elijah"* and he outran the king's chariot pulled by strong horses (1 Kings 18:46 NIV). Elijah outran the most quality means of travel in his day. This verse gives us a small picture of one of the many ways we can experience spiritual travel—but it all begins with this "on" dimension of the Holy Spirit.

In the Old Testament this phenomenon of supernatural abilities is mentioned over and over. It's mentioned in many different ways. The hand of God came on Elisha when the minstrel played and empowered him to prophesy. David even went into further detail of this event when he described his head being anointed with oil, causing what was in him to flow out. When the Holy Spirit comes on us, the divine nature in us comes alive and flows out of us.

The Spirit coming upon someone is always used in the context of accomplishing an assignment God gave them. In my life, whenever I'm preaching and truly imbued by the Holy Spirit, I feel His Spirit come on me about an hour before the meeting. I'm not just operating what's inside me. Each dimension upgrades our ability. When I'm flowing only in my infilling, healings, miracles, and other things do happen. However, when He comes on me, my voice changes, my boldness changes, and everything in me goes to another level.

The Bible says that when the Spirit came on Saul, he was transformed into another man—from Saul the enemy of Christians to Paul the champion of God's people (see Acts 9:1-31). In my experience God has certainly been transforming me into the image and likeness of Christ. There have actually been times when I become unrecognizable. Many people are shocked when they meet me off the pulpit because I look so different from who they see while I minister. I'm very quiet naturally; but when the Holy Spirit comes on me, I go from power, to great power. I go from grace, to great grace.

WITH THE HOLY SPIRIT, YOU GO FROM POWER TO GREAT POWER, AND FROM GRACE TO GREAT GRACE.

Another great truth is that the *infilling* does not increase or decrease. God does not give you a different amount of the Holy Spirit from another person. But what's *on* you can increase and decrease. When the Spirit comes, He comes with impartation. That's why the Bible says *"with* great power *the apostles gave witness to the resurrection of the Lord Jesus. And great grace was upon them all"* (Acts 4:33 NKJV). The power and grace on them had increased from what they first had.

Right now, I declare that what God has placed on you would increase. We are about to go from miracles, to notable miracles, from works, to greater works, from one amount of power to another, from one faith to another faith, and from glory to glory.

In Luke 24:49 we see an example of this supernatural upgrade of power and grace. Jesus told His disciples that they will be *"endued with power from on high."* This dimension of the Holy Spirit's work clothes you with what is needed to defeat the enemy. In my experience, this aspect of God's power does not remain active permanently; for example, in seasons when I press into God's glory, I carry more glory on my life.

Ezekiel 37:1 says that the hand of the Lord came on the prophet Ezekiel and brought him to the valley of dry bones. Once again this is another example of the Holy Spirit coming on someone and empowering him to travel by the spiritual realm. I believe that even the seven spirits of God are connected to this dimension of the Holy Spirit because the Scriptures tell us that the eyes of the Lord go to and fro searching for someone to show Himself strong.

Seven Spirits of God

According to Scripture we know that the eyes of the Lord are referenced as the seven spirits of God (see Isaiah 11:2). This means that the seven spirits search for people who are willing and available to be used by God as we move with God on us, and He empowers us. The seven spirits of God are: the Spirit of the Lord, Spirit of wisdom, the Spirit of understanding, the Spirit of counsel, the Spirit of might/strength, the Spirit of knowledge, and the Spirit of the fear of the Lord. There are not seven Holy Spirits—these seven spirits that comprise the fullness of the Holy Spirit. And He is searching the earth for someone through whom He can work great signs and wonders.

Psalm 147:11 (NIV) says *"the Lord delights in those who fear him, who put their hope in his unfailing love."* Fear in this case is translated reverence, respect, or reverential awe. So we could say that God is delighted when we come before Him in reverential awe. Loosely, the meaning is comparable to holy respect. I believe that understanding the fear of the Lord will help us unlock greater access into the glory realms, and walking in the seven spirits of God. Three times in the psalms we are told that *"The fear of the Lord is the beginning of wisdom and knowledge"* (Proverbs 1:7; 9:10; Psalm 111:10. Notice that wisdom and knowledge both begin with the fear of the Lord. This means that the fear of the Lord serves as a foundation that brings us into other realms.

Walking with God brings with it a healthy fear of the Lord—respect and reverential awe of the Almighty. Many people want the supernatural without the fear of God and it's why many end up in a different, sometimes dangerous spirit. When you have the fear of the Lord, you will walk in the seven spirits of God. This is why the eyes of the Lord are searching for people whose hearts are made perfect toward Him. In scripture, when we see the glory, we often see the fear of the Lord.

Glory of God

As mentioned previously, Luke 9 tells us that Jesus was transfigured and His face and clothes began to radiate the glory of God; then a cloud manifested and Moses and Elijah talked with Him. Peter, James, and John witnessed what was happening; and when the Father spoke, they fell under the power and began to tremble because the fear of the Lord was present.

In Judges 6:21-23 the Angel of the Lord told Gideon not to fear. Why? It wasn't just the appearance of the Angel. It was because the Angel carried the very glory of God and the fear of the Lord was associated with that glory.

It's hard to ignore the fact that many times in Scripture where we see the glory of God, we also see the fear of the Lord's presence. In Acts 5, after Ananias and Sapphira died for lying in the glory of God to Peter, the result was an increase of the fear of the Lord—and after the fear of the Lord increased, there was an increase in the ministry of signs and wonders. The explosion of signs and wonders were directly associated with the fear of the Lord. We must have the fear of the Lord to step into realms of glory.

The Bible even says in Psalm 34:7 that angels encamp round about those who fear Him. We will even see an increase of angelic activity as we begin to walk in the ministry of the glory of God. We will touch more on this as we cover the last dimension of walking in the Spirit.

The Bible says in Second Chronicles 16:9 that the eyes of the Lord go to and fro searching for those to whom He can show Himself strong because the seven spirits of God come upon us and then lift off. When we refer to the power of God coming on us, that power remains on us while we are doing the Lord's work and when He has assignments for us. The Holy Spirit in us is constant, the power of God on us is not. Elijah couldn't outrun chariots whenever he wanted to; that was a power that came on him for that particular assignment God gave him. It is the same for us.

The Spirit With You

Now let's focus on the last dimension of walking with the Holy Spirit and that is the dimension called God *with* us. I believe that we actually see all three dimensions take place in the life of the early church in the upper room—recorded in Acts 2. I say this because if we take a close look at each verse in Acts 2 we will see that the fire of God came on the disciples and filled them. Afterward we see that the Holy Spirit began to work with them. The Holy Spirit *began* to work with them, as they didn't go out and evangelize the three thousand (Acts 2:41). In fact no one did anything to make those individuals show up; it was simply a work of the Holy Spirit being with them (see also Acts 2:46-47).

This is what happens when we walk in the three dimensions of the Holy Spirit. The early church was completely submerged in the Holy Spirit and fire and then they walked out all three of the dimensions. Mark 16 tells us that the disciples preached the gospel everywhere, and the Holy Spirit was working with them.

Using an example from the Azusa Street Revival, it was said that three blocks away from the Azusa Street Mission—where the revival was taking place—people would suddenly be gripped and pulled toward the revival and they didn't know why. Of course, the Holy Spirit was actively working among them.

The Holy Spirit is the best Evangelist. I believe the Welsh Revival can also be used an example. This revival took place in Wales with the young Evan Roberts in the lead and caused a supernatural awareness of God in the entire nation when many surrendered their lives to the lordship of Jesus. In just a short period of time, more than one hundred thousand people were saved. Also, the revival affected everything—all the businesses, sporting world, and even the politics of the country. Everyone's priority was revival. Heaven had engulfed the nation in its flame.

Despite all the worldwide means of communication today, we can't honestly say that we see the type of results that were once seen during previous efforts.

In the previous "Spirit on" dimension of the Holy Spirit, God uses us to demonstrate His power. In this "Spirit with" dimension, God is at work around us. An example is when people brought sick people on the street where Peter was and his shadow healed them. Even though Ananias was used by God to minister to Paul while he was blind from the scales over his eyes, the Lord was at work strongly.

And no human could have preached the gospel to Paul, because he was too prideful and had hatred for Jesus in his heart. So God, who was working with the church, went to Paul himself; and in God's presence, Paul was changed to become one of the most committed believers of the New Testament. It's amusing to think that in God's presence, even the essence of stubbornness itself doesn't have a chance. That was only the beginning of Paul's transformation and his lifelong ministry. And, like Paul, we can be *"confident of this very thing, that He who has begun a good work in you will complete it until the day of Jesus Christ"* (Philippians 1:6 NKJV). Amen and amen and amen!

Prayer

Father God,

In Jesus' name, I thank You for Your Spirit being in me, on me, and with me. Holy Spirit, I ask to know You in every dimension. I pray for the fullness of Your Spirit. And I pray, Holy Spirit, that You will continue to work in my heart and my life until the day I see You face to face or until the day of Your glorious return. Amen.

9

RIVERS OF OIL

Oh, that I were as in months past, as in the days
when God watched over me; when His lamp shone
upon my head, and when by His light I walked
through darkness; just as I was in the days of my
prime, when the friendly counsel of God was over
my tent; when the Almighty was yet with me,
when my children were around me; when my
steps were bathed with cream, and the rock poured
out rivers of oil for me! (Job 29:1-6 NKJV)

I must have it! This was the thought that ran through my head
when I read about Smith Wigglesworth. Something in me

stirred as I read that he raised the dead. I could not shake the divine hunger I felt rising inside me as I read of the power of God working through Wigglesworth. I was like Habakkuk when he prayed that he heard of God's fame and *"I stand in awe of Your deeds, Lord. Repeat them in our day, in our time make them known…"* (Habakkuk 3:2 NIV).

God's Anointing—Past, Current, Future

This is what revival should do. Revival should bring back to life the deeds of God seen in previous generations of God's people. The real anointing should not be any less than what the anointing was in the Bible. When the anointing came on people, nothing about them was ordinary any longer. A generation is rising that will move in all of the supernatural of God.

God instructed His people to tell the testimonies of His miracles, signs, and wonders in the past. After all, if you don't know the works of God, you can't believe them, which leads to a lack of hunger. Wherever the supernatural is lacking, the result is a lukewarm and dead people.

The first key to walking in the types of anointings that shook cities and nations is to become hungry. Hunger is a spiritual principle. This is why the Bible tells us to desire spiritual gifts. In the spirit, you attract what you are hungry for—the law of hunger and thirst. When you *"hunger and thirst for righteousness,"* you will be filled and blessed (Matthew 5:6).

I have never met anyone who moves in the gifts of the Spirit powerfully who was not hungry to receive the gifts. I have also never met anyone who has been anointed by the Spirit who wasn't in the realm of hunger. We must become hungry to see the God of Abraham, Isaac, and Jacob. We must see the God of Moses, Peter, and Paul. We must be anointed like those we read about in Scripture. Are you going to be that next person God anoints to change a generation?

There are several aspects of the anointing that we must learn. Job 29:6 tells us that Job's feet were bathed with cream, or butter, and God poured rivers of oil from the rock. This verse reveals two principles—the anointing is diverse and the anointing makes things easier. The anointing can't produce any results beyond its measure and it cannot produce outside of the type of anointing it is.

WHATEVER YOUR DESTINY, AN ANOINTING WILL BRING YOU INTO THE FULLNESS OF YOUR CALLING AND SPHERE OF INFLUENCE.

There are many types of anointings and one anointing doesn't enable you to do everything. It's very important to discover what type of anointing is in your life because if you don't, your attempts will yield no results. I have accepted that I am not anointed for everything. I also have learned to recognize when something is also beyond my authority in the level of anointing I am in. Many people believe that the entire corporate Body of Christ is called to be anointed on three levels, the prophet, the priest, and the king. This doesn't mean that every believer will be a prophet, but it does mean that every believer will partake in a measure of the prophetic anointing, be able to hear the voice of God, and operate in the gifts of the Spirit.

The priestly anointing is the anointing to minister to the Lord, enter His presence, and have access into the very glory of God. The kingly anointing, I believe, is the specific anointing for the special assignment and call of each individual member of the Body of Christ.

For some, the kingly anointing may be for business, for others it may be for arts and entertainment, or perhaps politics. We may also see the kingly anointing establish a fivefold ministry in their specific office. I'm not saying that the kingly anointing is exactly the same anointing on every believer.

Whatever our destiny, there is a kind and measure of anointing that brings us into the fullness of our callings and the sphere of influence to which we are called. God doesn't aimlessly pour out the anointing. It comes with a purpose—and the kind of oil God gives us is connected to what we need divine empowerment for. If we are not called to speak to nations as a prophet, the anointing will not promote us into a function that provides a platform to speak to kings and queens or prime ministers or presidents. The anointing is not given to us to become famous. God will never pour the level of oil beyond the level of assignment, and He will not give us a kind of anointing that is not needed for our specific tasks.

The Fullness of Anointing

We can ask God to increase the anointing; but remember, Jesus didn't ask for a new anointing after the Spirit came on

Him like a dove and remained. When Jesus was baptized, He received the full measure of the anointing. That was the moment when the Father released Jesus into the fullness of His ministry; therefore, giving Him the fullness of the anointing He would need for the task. The three times David was anointed brought him into the full measure of his anointing needed for his kingly office:

> *So Samuel took the horn of oil and anointed him in the presence of his brothers, and from that day on the Spirit of the Lord came powerfully upon David. Samuel then went to Ramah* (1 Samuel 16:13 NIV).
>
> *Then the men of Judah came to Hebron, and there they anointed David king over the tribe of Judah...* (2 Samuel 2:4 NIV).
>
> *All the tribes of Israel came to David at Hebron and said, "We are your own flesh and blood. In the past, while Saul was king over us, you were the one who led Israel on their military campaigns. And the Lord said to you, 'You will shepherd my people Israel, and you will become their ruler.'" When all the elders of Israel had come to King David at Hebron, the king made a covenant with them at Hebron before the Lord, and they anointed David king over Israel. David was thirty years old when he became king, and he reigned forty years. In Hebron he reigned over Judah seven years and six months, and in Jerusalem he reigned over all Israel and Judah thirty-three years* (2 Samuel 5:1-5 NIV).

Notice that in each of the times that David was anointed, the first time was the only time that mentioned the Spirit coming powerfully upon David. This is because the Holy Spirit Himself did not increase—the anointing increased, promoting David into greater authority within his God-given assignment each time.

Today many people believe that they can bypass paying a price; but the truth is, even with impartation, you will never reach the fullness of the anointing without paying a price. Even when we see the seven men filled with the Holy Spirit that the apostles laid hands on, these men were already full of the Holy Spirit when they laid hands on them. The results seen in the life of Philip and Stephen did not come simply because hands were laid on them. It was because they were already men who had a strong relationship with the Holy Spirit.

In those days when the number of disciples was increasing, the Hellenistic Jews among them complained against the Hebraic Jews because their widows were being overlooked in the daily distribution of food. So the Twelve gathered all the disciples together and said, "It would not be right for us to neglect the ministry of the word of God in order to wait on tables. Brothers and sisters, choose seven men from among you who are known to be full of the Spirit and wisdom. We'll turn this responsibility over to them and will give our attention to prayer and the ministry of the word" (Acts 6:1-4 NIV).

Notice that the apostles searched for men who were known to be full of the Holy Spirit. The results speak for themselves.

> *Now Stephen, a man full of God's grace and power, performed great wonders and signs among the people. Opposition arose, however, from members of the Synagogue of the Freedmen (as it was called)—Jews of Cyrene and Alexandria as well as the provinces of Cilicia and Asia—who began to argue with Stephen. But they could not stand up against the wisdom the Spirit gave him as he spoke* (Acts 6:8-10 NIV).

> *Those who had been scattered preached the word wherever they went. Philip went down to a city in Samaria and proclaimed the Messiah there. When the crowds heard Philip and saw the signs he performed, they all paid close attention to what he said. For with shrieks, impure spirits came out of many, and many who were paralyzed or lame were healed. So there was great joy in that city* (Acts 8:4-8 NIV).

The anointing on you operates at its highest potential when you are full of the Spirit. This is why we can see a connection between the anointing and the Holy Spirit.

> *How God anointed Jesus of Nazareth with the Holy Spirit and with power, who went about doing good and healing all who were oppressed by the devil, for God was with Him* (Acts 10:38 NKJV).

With a close examination of Acts 10:38, we can see two dimensions being keys to Jesus operating in healing and deliverance—the Holy Spirit's presence and power. When the Holy

Spirit comes on you, He activates or stirs what's inside you. We first receive an anointing directly from the Holy Spirit's presence; and second, we receive power from the Holy Spirit.

Many people want the anointing without having the presence of God. We must learn how to seek and value the presence of Jesus. Anyone who doesn't value the presence of the Holy Spirit will never be able to sustain any anointing of the Holy Spirit.

NO PRESENCE OF GOD—NO ANOINTING.

Many ministers who lose their *"first love"* (Revelation 2:4 NKJV) will have only a residue of the power compared to the time when they deeply loved Jesus. Though some may eventually become false ministers and people who represent only themselves in ministry, this can also happen to any believer who simply becomes too lazy to pay the price to steward the oil that God has given them.

The power of God can be manifested in healing grace, miracle grace, prosperity and financial grace, prophetic grace, grace for media, grace for writing, grace for preaching, and many other aspects of the grace of God. We can refer to these as different rivers of oil.

So to reiterate—one dimension of the anointing comes directly from the presence of the Holy Spirit, while the other is the specific power given based on what's needed at the time. This power is given in two different ways:

1. Sometimes the power comes onto a person and then lifts after completion of the assignment.

2. The power can also come into an atmosphere and then lift as well.

When people operate in the power of God one of these ways, they may not see the same results as frequently as when someone receives a mantle.

Mantles and Anointings

The mantle is packed with anointing, gifts, and even opens realms of influence in order to empower a person's ministry. For example, an apostolic mantle is not the same as an apostolic anointing. The *apostolic mantle* has within it the working of miracles, gifts of healings, and the gifts of faith, along with a sustained apostolic anointing. A person with an *apostolic anointing* often gains that anointing through relationship and impartation to an apostle. This is what the Bible means when it says that these particular ministries equip the Body for the work of ministry in Ephesians 4. The mantle does not lose its power, but if a person does not walk in intimacy with the Holy Spirit, the power within the mantle can go dormant and will need to be awakened or stirred up.

I remember the first time I experienced the anointing of the Holy Spirit coming on me in a recognizable way and activating something within me. I grew up very shy and reserved. I kept a very small circle of friends and was extremely uncomfortable talking in front of people. I struggled with this fear so badly that I would even avoid crowded restaurants and large gatherings. I just couldn't get past the feelings of rejection that stemmed from childhood. Even as a teenager in church, I would have panic attacks when asked to read Scriptures in front of the church.

I'm explaining this to tell you that when the anointing of the Spirit comes on you, you become a different person. The day I experienced His anointing come upon me for the first time, it changed me forever. I was at a prayer service and had been born again for about a year at the time. The prayer leader wanted us all to learn how to pray with a microphone that projected our voices. I wish I could tell you how I was so ready to rise up and pray, but I was terrified. I remember feeling a paralyzing fear. I needed deliverance, but that's for another book. The prayer leader gave prayer targets to each of us, and then one by one she asked us to go up front and pray while holding the microphone.

I watched as each person went up and prayed and wondered when my time would come. *Perhaps she knows I'm not ready and is letting the stronger, more qualified people pray first,* I thought. Then after everyone had prayed, she called my name, "CHAZ!" She gave me my prayer target and I was shaking with fear as I walked forward; then I stood at the podium with my head down.

And that's when it happened!

When I opened my mouth, the sound of the Lion of Judah spoke. Power and fire filled the atmosphere and I didn't recognize my voice. The apostolic/prophetic sound thundering out of me was nothing I had experienced personally. As I heard my voice change, I became more and more bold. My mannerisms changed, no longer was I looking down at my shoes. I was pointing my finger and wildly waving, standing tall. *Am I dreaming?* I wondered.

When I came back to myself, everyone was in awe. The quiet guy who rarely talked had gone from being Clark Kent to Superman. My pastor at the time ran out of his office to see who was praying and he was utterly shocked when he saw it was me. Everyone saw God's anointing empowering me for His work.

You too can become unrecognizable as the anointing of the Holy Spirit operates upon you. You may not seem like much in the eyes of others, but like Moses, Gideon, and many more, God's anointing will empower you to reach your destiny.

Power and Authorization

The anointing is not only the power of God to fulfill a ministry, it can also be the very authorization for which the anointing was released. When we look at Aaron and his sons being anointed into the priesthood, we see that the anointing authorized them to function as priests, as well as empowered them to be effective. Very often in Scripture we see a prophet anoint a king. This act not only gave the king supernatural ability, it also authorized them to function as a king.

We see an example of this with Solomon and Adonijah in First Kings 1. When David was old and about to pass away. His son Adonijah was the oldest son due to Absolom passing away. He assumed that he would instantly be made king as the oldest and illegally made himself king before David had announced who would sit on the throne. As I read this historical account in Scripture, I immediately noticed that Adonijah was never anointed as king.

As the story continues, eventually Nathan the prophet informs David what was happening. Solomon's mother just so happened to be talking to King David about the situation as well. David then made it official. He advised that Solomon would be king. He also advised that Nathan and Zadok the priest anoint him as king.

> There let Zadok the priest and Nathan the prophet anoint him king over Israel; and blow the horn, and say, "Long live King Solomon!" Then you shall come up after him, and he shall come and sit on my throne, and he shall be king in my place. For I have appointed him to be ruler over Israel and Judah (1 Kings 1:34-35 NKJV).

Adonijah's kingship was fraudulent. Similar to a stolen election. The anointing is not only power—it's authorization. Adonijah was not anointed, so God was not involved in Adonijah's actions. Because Solomon was anointed, he was lifted in honor and known for his wisdom (1 Kings 4:29-34) and given authority and a long life.

Prayer

Father,

Right now in the name of Jesus, I thank You for pouring Your rivers of oil on me. I ask for the Holy Spirit to come upon my life and anoint me. Give me the grace of God to accomplish everything I'm called by You to do. Lord, bathe me in Your oil and completely soak my life. Let the power of God flow through me to others. Let me be a witness of the truth that Jesus rose from the dead. In Jesus' name, amen.

10

GLORY DIMENSIONS

They said, "Look, the Lord our God has shown
us his glory and greatness, and we have heard
his voice from the heart of the fire. Today we
have seen that God can speak to us humans,
and yet we live!" (Deuteronomy 5:24 NLT)

There are many dimensions of the glory of God—so many that no definition can ever completely describe the fullness of His glory. The multifaceted glory of God must be experienced time and time again. Each definition is a dimension we can experience, and has levels upon levels of reality. Consequently, I don't make the focus of this chapter on the different definitions of the word "glory"—rather, that would fill a book.

Many are accustomed to hearing about the dimension of the glory that the priest experienced when he couldn't stand in Solomon's temple because of how heavy the glory became (2 Chronicles 7). They conclude that if the glory of God is present, everyone will fall to the ground. I used to believe this as well, until one day I was reading about Jesus turning water into wine (John 2:1-12). After Jesus turned the water into wine, the Scripture tells us that it was a manifestation of His glory, yet no one fell. It's not recorded that anyone who drank the wine could not stand up; therefore, we can ascertain that the people were just in awe of the taste. The governor of the feast stated that they had saved the best wine for last.

These are examples of how God's glory can manifest in many ways. The glory in Solomon's temple is a different facet of the glory from when Jesus turned water into wine. It would be a huge mistake for us to assume that the glory will always look the same.

Jesus was the glory in a human body. We see Him take several different forms in Scripture where He was not recognizable, even by people who were often with Jesus. Just think of when Jesus walked on the water and His disciples thought He was a ghost, or when Jesus rose from the dead and talked with two of His disciples who didn't recognize Him (Luke 24). A truth we often miss is that Jesus *is* the glory.

The Bible says that the fullness of God dwells inside His human body. Jesus is the radiant glory of the Father. If we seek the presence of Jesus with all of our heart, we will always find ourselves in His glory. As you read on, I don't want you to lose the heart of this chapter—experiencing Jesus is experiencing glory.

Three Dimensions

We don't have to seek signs and wonders. We don't have to see glory clouds and pray for gold dust to appear. We simply have to seek Jesus; and as we do, we remain sensitive and alert to notice the signs and wonders of His glory following us. Glory is commonly described using three primary words that seem best to describe all the fullness of the supernatural glory, which reveal three dimensions of glory: 1) Kobod; 2) Shekinah; and 3) Doxa. Now let's look closely at each of the three.

Kobod

Kobod is weighty or heavy glory. We see this glory demonstrated when people could not stand under the weight of His glory (Numbers 20:6; Ezekiel 1:28; 3:23; 44:4). When John the beloved fell as dead when he saw Jesus like the sun shining in its strength in Revelation chapter 1. Another example is when Abraham fell down and worshipped God in Genesis 24:48. Kobod was and is weighty glory.

One of the greatest examples of this is when Solomon dedicated the temple to the Lord. God responded by releasing a heavy glory that knocked the priests down and seemed to pin them on the floor. They couldn't stand to minister.

This glory will not instantly knock us down, but I believe these are great examples of this particular dimension. When we experience the Kobod glory, it comes in measures. Think of it as God adding weight to the atmosphere and upon us progressively as we minister to Him.

Shekinah

The Shekinah glory of God is not actually a word found in the Bible. It was the Jewish rabbi who used this word to describe aspects of the glory of God, which means the dwelling place of glory. It seems to be used in the context of visible glory. In Scripture, a great example is the cloud by day and the pillar of fire by night that led the Israelites during the exodus from Egypt (Exodus 13:21-22).

Shekinah glory is often used to describe gold dust as well. I remember the first time I experienced this phenomenon. Gold dust came out of my pores during my prayer time. The following day, my prayer room was covered in gold dust. The Lord spoke to me, "This is a sign of new realms of glory." I don't believe this is what it means every time, though. Signs are a form of the voice of God speaking to us.

After this initial experience, we have consistently seen this sign in our ministry. Sometimes it pours out of my wife and I, and we are covered with it after services. People in our gathering can often see the glory on their hands. We even experienced gold dust raining down in my office. We have also on a few occasions witnessed a visible glory cloud form. The strongest I have seen it was actually during a deliverance service. As the cloud came into the atmosphere, many demons were cast out and I even saw the cloud on social media recordings.

Doxa

The word "Doxa" speaks of the judgment and the view we have of another person. In the context of spiritual glory, it is a glory that reveals who God is. In other words Doxa is revelatory glory; glory that comes to reveal the character of God. For example, God is loving, merciful, holy, good, just, omniscient, faithful…. Many Scriptures throughout the Bible verify these, as well as many other righteous character traits of our heavenly Father. I encourage you to search the Bible and take note of all you find.

We have been called to move in the glory; however, we must distinguish the glory of God from several other dimensions of God. We must first distinguish presence versus power. Then we must differentiate between faith, the anointing of God, and then the glory of God. The Bible says that Jesus was anointed with the Holy Spirit and power—because there is a difference between the presence and power of God. When Jesus breathed on the disciples and they received the Holy Spirit, they instantly received His presence. However, they had to wait to receive power in the upper room (this was discussed in Chapter 8).

Many believers today are people of the presence of God, but they are yet to know His power. You can attend ministries and enjoy the beautiful presence of God in worship, but not see any demonstration of His power. It's not that they are wrong. They have just settled for presence and haven't sought the power. Imagine if the one hundred and twenty disciples never went to the upper room because they thought it was enough that they had already received the Holy Spirit when Jesus breathed on them. How tragic that would have been!

WE NEED GOOD CHARACTER AND THE POWER OF GOD.

Some even make claims that all we need is character. This is erroneous thinking. Jesus was a Man of both character *and* the power of God. People with this mindset assume that because they experience the sweet presence of God that they need nothing else. What they fail to understand is that God's power is not His Person.

Please understand this truth clearly. A believer who no longer knows the presence of Jesus, can continue to move in His power on some level. *Really?* you may wonder. Well, consider this Bible passage when Jesus says:

> *Not everyone who says to me, "Lord, Lord," will enter the kingdom of heaven, but only the one who does the will of my Father who is in heaven. Many will say to me on that day, "Lord, Lord, did we not prophesy in your name and in your name drive out demons and in your name perform many miracles?" Then I will tell them plainly, "I never knew you. Away from me, you evildoers!"* (Matthew 7:21-23 NIV).

Jesus was talking about people who lost the presence of God, but power remained operating in their lives. This further validates that presence and power are two different dimensions of the glory.

With that understanding as a foundation, it is easier to now understand that the gifts can be in operation, but it doesn't mean we are in the glory. We need to make these distinctions to gain individual understanding of each. We must also know that all of these dimensions work together and are meant to connect as one to bring us into the fullness of God.

I believe that to enter into the glory, we must begin with faith, enter the anointing, and then we will see manifested glory.

The Realm of Faith

I explain this progression into glory through faith. Notice that in Scripture going from faith to faith, is connected to going from glory to glory (2 Corinthians 3:18). Before you can begin to operate in the anointing or operating in the glory, you must first enter the realms of faith. Faith is the way to enter, receive, and experience all of the supernatural. The Bible defines faith as the substance of what's hoped for and the evidence of things not seen (Hebrews 11:1 NKJV). I want to draw your attention to the fact that Hebrews 11:1 says faith is a substance, and faith is part of the invisible world. So faith is a tangible substance in the supernatural realm.

FAITH IS A TANGIBLE SUBSTANCE IN THE SUPERNATURAL REALM.

This means that faith is not only to believe, it's when God's world is revealed to us. The more revelation God gives us, the more faith we receive. This is why the Bible says faith comes by hearing (Romans 10:17). Faith is directly connected to the operation of our spiritual senses. Romans 10:17 describes how when we hear the voice of God, faith is imparted through hearing. So, faith is based on revelation or insight into the spiritual made known to us. Faith is not just to believe, it's to believe because of what has been revealed to us.

A great example of this can be seen in First Corinthians 2:9-10 (NIV):

> *However, as it is written: "What no eye has seen, what no ear has heard, and what no human mind has conceived"—the things God has prepared for those who love him—these are the things God has revealed to us by his Spirit. The Spirit searches all things, even the deep things of God.*

God has things in the spiritual realm that the natural eyes and natural ears can't hear or see. Things that have been prepared already in Spirit form. The Holy Spirit in us searches these things out; and as they are made known to us, faith rises in our heart to bring them to pass through prayer and actions that align with what's in the Spirit.

TO LIVE IN TRUE FAITH, WE MUST LIVE BY WHAT GOD MAKES KNOWN TO US.

So when the Scriptures say that we shall live by faith and not sight, it's essentially saying we are to live by our spiritual senses, not our natural ones. To live in true faith, we must live by what God makes known to us—naturally and supernaturally.

Faith is also a foundation in the spiritual realm. This is why *"faith toward God"* is listed among the foundational principles:

> *Therefore, leaving the discussion of the elementary principles of Christ, let us go on to perfection, not laying again the foundation of repentance from dead works and of faith toward God* (Hebrews 6:1 NKJV).

I love how it says, *"faith toward."* This means that we can put our faith toward something. First, of course, we must learn to put our faith toward God. Because the focus of this book isn't on faith, I don't cover this topic in detail; however, faith must be applied when entering the supernatural—such as faith must be involved in the release of God's power through us.

Here is a key to faith—faith is imparted when God reveals to us what He wants us to know. Then our faith can be activated over and over again in the area where we have the wisdom to know how to apply it. So in reference to us entering or activating our faith when entering the spiritual realm, activating the anointing on us, and transitioning into God's glory, we must spiritually understand what prayer, praise, and worship do supernaturally. We don't cover this topic extensively, just enough to convey the message of this chapter on the dimensions of glory.

The Anointing

When we enter the realm of faith, we can continue transitioning deeper until we enter into the realm of the anointing. Whatever stirred our faith, if we do more of it, we will find ourselves moving with God into His anointing. You can't have the glory of God without first having His anointing. Though there is a chapter on the anointing that you already read in this book, I want to now discuss the anointing in regard to its connection to the process of entering the glory realm. The anointing can be absorbed into an atmosphere.

This is what Luke 5:17 (NKJV) means when it says that *"the power of the Lord was present to heal them."* The healing anointing had filled the very air they were breathing. The powerful thing about this realm is that the faith required to begin the process of entering into the anointing is still in operation—and this same thing happens in the glory.

Each dimension adds to the next, leading to an increase of whatever God was doing in the previous dimension. If I pray for ten people by faith, a smaller number of them will be healed; but when I pray by the anointing, the results increase. In the glory, there are no limits. We must discern the reason the glory manifested.

Open Heavens and Glory

Enter into His gates with thanksgiving, and into His courts with praise. Be thankful to Him, and bless His name (Psalm 100:4 NKJV).

A hidden revelation can be found within this very short verse in Psalm 100. It is a divine blueprint that opens the supernatural if we follow its pattern. David tells us to *"Enter into His gates with thanksgiving."* When we praise in thanksgiving, the atmosphere changes. We begin to feel the presence of God saturating our environment. Giving thanks to God opens spiritual gates. These gates serve as access points for Heaven to flood into the natural world. As we praise Him, the gates open and we can enter the spirit world, or the spiritual realm.

The Bible also tells us how to go deeper into the spirit. We know that the tabernacle had three courts and was patterned after the heavenly tabernacle. When Moses led Israel in its construction, God showed him what He wanted it to look like—it was to be an earthly replica of the tabernacle in the supernatural realm. This physical tabernacle on earth had three courts and many believe the courts represented the three dimensions of the spirit—faith, anointing, and glory.

THE ATMOSPHERE REVEALS SPIRITUAL ACTIVITY.

As we praise and the portals open, if we continue to praise Him with thankfulness in our heart and with passion, we will experience the next part of the Psalm 100:4. We will *"enter into His courts."* We will move from the outer court to the inner court, and then into the most holy place where the glory is. You may not visibly see anything while you are entering His gates with thanksgiving and praise, but you will notice more and more a change in the atmosphere. Remember that atmospheres reveal spiritual activity.

I believe this correlates to what Ruth Ward Heflin famously said, "Praise until worship comes, worship until the glory comes, and then stand in the glory." Living in the glory is to become someone who worships the Father with radical passion, which becomes the gate into the glory and a throne for God's glory to sit upon. He is enthroned by our praise and worship (Psalm 22:3 NKJV). Ministries known for the glory of God place special emphasis on praise and worship.

Giving can bring us into powerful dimensions of the glory of God. In Malachi 3:8-10, the heavens open as the Bible mentions our tithes and our offerings. Giving is a powerful way to open supernatural windows. Before I go further into this, I want to detail a few powerful aspects about how God designed the heavens to access the earth.

John 10 describes entering the spirit realm in the context of illegal doors. Jesus said that if anyone enters through any other door they are thieves and robbers. John 10:3 mentions a doorkeeper who opens the door, which tells us that the world of the supernatural has access points that guide us into the invisible world.

Access points mentioned in the Bible are altars, gates, windows, and doors and all serve the same purpose—for the glory of God to manifest on earth, to connect Heaven and earth. When we learn how to open the heavens, we can experience God's supernatural activity in our day-to-day lives. Let's look at each one.

Altars

Then God said to Jacob, "Get ready and move to Bethel and settle there. Build an altar there to the God who appeared to you when you fled from your brother, Esau" (Genesis 35:1 NLT).

Altars are symbolic and spiritual covenants. In Genesis 28:16-19, Jacob has an encounter with God:

> *Then Jacob awoke from his sleep and said, "Surely the Lord is in this place, and I wasn't even aware of it!" But he was also afraid and said, "What an awesome place this is! It is none other than the house of God, the very gateway to heaven!" The next morning Jacob got up very early. He took the stone he had rested his head against, and he set it upright as a memorial pillar. Then he poured olive oil over it. He named that place Bethel (which means "house of God"), although it was previously called Luz.* (Genesis 28:16-19 NLT).

It is obvious that these Scripture passages in Genesis clearly show how Heaven's activity is very much connected to what we do on earth. The very place that Jacob laid down was where Abraham had raised an altar to God (Genesis 12:7-8). Even though the physical altar no longer stood, in the spiritual realm, that altar remained and served as a covenant that affected multiple generations. The altar opened a constant flow of divine access between Heaven and earth.

This is what the modern-day church should also be in our regions. Our churches are called to be places from which revival glory can flow. Altars regulate what comes in and out and serves as gates that give access or deny access. This is why Jesus told Peter that the gates of hell would not prevail against the church (Matthew 16:18). Immediately after this statement, Jesus tells Peter, *"whatever you bind on earth will be bound in heaven, and whatever you loose on earth will be loosed in heaven"* (Matthew 16:19 NKJV). Jesus was telling Peter that His church will be a gate that determines what comes in and out of the spirit world. Wherever there are apostolic/prophetic ministries, there will be a wide-open gate within the realm of influence assigned to that ministry.

Gates

The Bible says in Psalm 24:7 (NKJV): *"Lift up your heads, O you gates! And be lifted up, you everlasting doors! And the King of glory shall come in."* In the natural, ancient world, cities had many gates. Jerusalem had twelve gates. In the spiritual realm, all nations, states, regions, cities, communities, ministries, families, and individuals have gates.

Psalm 24 shows us that the function of these lifted up and opened gates is to allow entry for the King of glory to come in. We see this simple principle over and over through all these access points that we are discussing. When they are open, the glory realm can flood in. Though altars become gates, they are slightly different.

Windows

The Scriptures speak of windows of Heaven. When Heaven's windows are opened, the Bible says that blessings will be poured out—so much so that there is not enough room to receive them all.

> *"Bring all the tithes into the storehouse so there will be enough food in my Temple. If you do," says the Lord of Heaven's Armies, "I will open the windows of heaven for you. I will pour out a blessing so great you won't*

have enough room to take it in! Try it! Put me to the test!" (Malachi 3:10 NLT)

Doors

Revelation 4:1 details a spiritual door that John saw in Heaven. He then heard God speak to him and invite him up, and as he entered it would open greater vision. God told John that he would see things that must shortly come to pass when he accepted the invitation. As these doors open we will see greater glory. John was already in Heaven but he was invited into a greater dimension of Heaven. He had to look up to see the door. He entered a "Heaven above the Heaven."

> *Then as I looked, I saw a door standing open in heaven, and the same voice I had heard before spoke to me like a trumpet blast. The voice said, "Come up here, and I will show you what must happen after this"* (Revelation 4:1 NLT).

In Revelation 3, Jesus *"opens a door that no one shuts, and shuts and no one opens: I know your works. See, I have set before you an open door, and no one can shut it..."* (Revelation 3:7-8 NKJV). God follows His own protocols. We must be the ones who have *"obeyed my command to persevere, I will protect you from the great time of testing that will come upon the whole world to test those who belong to this world. I am coming soon. Hold on to what you have, so that no one will take away your crown. All who are victorious will become pillars in the Temple of my God, and they will never have to leave it. And I will write on them the name of my God, and they will be citizens in the city of my God—the new Jerusalem that comes down from heaven from my*

God. And I will also write on them my new names" (Revelation 3:10-12 NLT).

We can see open heavens in the book of Psalms in the way manna appeared every morning for Moses and the Israelites when they left Egypt.

Each access point is considered an open heaven. When the heavens are open, the glory of God manifests.

In 2019 we were in a service at our ministry in Jacksonville, Florida. Everyone was pouring themselves out passionately. This went on for close to an hour and the atmosphere was filled with the glory of God. As His heavy glory was increasing, a woman came forward and explained how she could now see out of her eye—although she had been blind in that eye since birth and doctors had performed two failed surgeries. Nevertheless, as she was worshipping in the manifested glory that day, the Lord healed her eye without anyone laying hands on her. As she testified, I even tried to lay hands on her to bless her, but she was slain in the Spirit even as I just walked near her. Praise God, she has been able to see ever since.

Resurrection Glory

Jesus' resurrection is so powerful that if we can grasp even a fraction of its impact, we would quickly see why it was the central message of the early church. Hidden within its reality is the very power that the early church moved in and advanced the gospel in unprecedented ways in the midst of a hostile world. The apostles flipped the world upside down because they understood how the cross and resurrection utterly defeated satan's kingdom. The cross reversed everything that satan had established by influencing the fall of humankind. As you gain this revelation, you too will affect the world around you with resurrection power!

To understand the resurrection of Jesus and its purpose, we must have a general understanding of the doctrine of resurrections, which is found in Hebrews 6:1. This doctrine can be put in four categories: 1) Jesus being raised from the dead; 2) the just being raised; 3) the unjust being raised; and then 4) the dead being raised through prayer. We will cover each one of these matters; and when we are finished, you will have a comprehensive understanding of being a child of God and what that truly means.

The Resurrection of Jesus

Jesus being raised from the dead was so extremely significant that the religious leaders tried to cover it up by saying that His disciples stole His body—to make it seem as if Jesus was not the Son of God as He claimed. Hell created a lie. Many other resurrections are recorded in the Bible—Lazarus, the little girl Jesus raised from the dead, Elijah raised the son of a widow— yet Jesus' resurrection was different. Why? Because:

> *Jesus said to her, "I am the resurrection and the life. He who believes in Me, though he may die, he shall live. And whoever lives and believes in Me shall never die. Do you believe this?" She said to Him, "Yes, Lord, I believe that You are the Christ, the Son of God, who is to come into the world"* (John 11:25-27 NKJV).

We know that even the Old Testament points to the revelation of Jesus—clearly in Isaiah 53 (NKJV):

Who has believed our report?
And to whom has the arm of the Lord been revealed?
For He shall grow up before Him as a tender plant,
And as a root out of dry ground.
He has no form or comeliness;
And when we see Him,
There is no beauty that we should desire Him.
He is despised and rejected by men,
A Man of sorrows and acquainted with grief.
And we hid, as it were, our faces from Him;
He was despised, and we did not esteem Him.
Surely He has borne our griefs
And carried our sorrows;
Yet we esteemed Him stricken,
Smitten by God, and afflicted.
But He was wounded for our transgressions,
He was bruised for our iniquities;
The chastisement for our peace was upon Him,
And by His stripes we are healed.
All we like sheep have gone astray;
We have turned, every one, to his own way;
And the Lord has laid on Him the iniquity of us all.
He was oppressed and He was afflicted,
Yet He opened not His mouth;

He was led as a lamb to the slaughter,

And as a sheep before its shearers is silent,

So He opened not His mouth.

He was taken from prison and from judgment,

And who will declare His generation?

For He was cut off from the land of the living;

For the transgressions of My people He was stricken.

And they made His grave with the wicked—

But with the rich at His death,

Because He had done no violence,

Nor was any deceit in His mouth.

Yet it pleased the Lord to bruise Him;

He has put Him to grief.

When You make His soul an offering for sin,

He shall see His seed, He shall prolong His days,

And the pleasure of the Lord shall prosper in His hand.

He shall see the labor of His soul, and be satisfied.

By His knowledge My righteous Servant shall justify many,

For He shall bear their iniquities.

Therefore I will divide Him a portion with the great,

And He shall divide the spoil with the strong,

Because He poured out His soul unto death,

And He was numbered with the transgressors,

And He bore the sin of many,

And made intercession for the transgressors.

Second Kings tells of a dead man being tossed into Elisha's tomb. Elisha had been dead long enough to completely decay. Only his bones remained. When the dead man's bones touched Elisha's, he was revived and came back to life.

> *So it was, as they were burying a man, that suddenly they spied a band of raiders; and they put the man in the tomb of Elisha; and when the man was let down and touched the bones of Elisha, he revived and stood on his feet* (2 Kings 13:21 NKJV).

This prophetically reveals the power that Jesus' death broke—the power of death and the grave! After the fall—after Adam and Eve disobeyed God—the dominion that God gave humankind was still intact. The issue was that we were separated from God and our nature had been corrupted. Satan understood that gaining access to humans and enslaving us would allow him to exercise dominion through us. The fact that humans were given rulership reveals why Jesus had to come in the flesh to save us from ourselves.

Jesus had to come to earth and live among us as a Man because dominion in the earth was delegated to us by His own design. Jesus would reverse what satan had accomplished and regain the authority that was lost. Consider how much integrity God has. He follows His own perfect and just laws. There is no one as holy as our God. He is truly a Man of His word.

So, Jesus was conceived by the Holy Spirit in Mary. Jesus received his DNA from Father God through the Spirit, yet He received humanity through Mary. This is how He is the

Son of God, yet human. Throughout His life Jesus never sinned—which leads us to the answer to our original question. Why was the resurrection of Jesus more significant than any other resurrection? The answer is in understanding DNA.

JESUS WAS WITHOUT SIN, SO HE RESURRECTED FROM THE GRAVE WITH THE VERY NATURE OF THE FATHER STILL IN HIM.

DNA was designed by God to pass on the nature of a creature to its offspring. This is why Adam's sin was so devastating. Every person after him would have a sin nature—a dead spirit. Others who were raised from the dead in Scripture rose with their sin nature still present in them. Because Jesus was without sin, He resurrected from the grave with the very nature of the Father still in Him.

The Spirit of Holiness

In Jesus' death, He took the very curse on Himself and experienced the wrath of God so that we did not have to. His resurrection proved that He is the Son of God, and declared Him to be the Son of God with power, according to the Spirit of holiness, by the resurrection from the dead (Romans 1:4).

In Scripture, the Pharisees were asking Jesus to perform a miracle to prove that He is the Son of God. Jesus' response to them was that only a wicked and adulterous generation seeks a sign and they won't have one except Jonah the prophet.

> *But Jesus replied, "Only an evil, adulterous generation would demand a miraculous sign; but the only sign I will give them is the sign of the prophet Jonah"* (Matthew 12:39 NLT).

Out of all the prophets in the Bible, why would Jesus choose the prophet who was so rebellious? Why did He not use Elijah or Moses? There are two reasons: 1) Jonah ministered to the Gentiles, representing all people; and 2), Jonah was in the belly of the fish for three days and nights. After three days, he was spit out of death's dark door into life. A foretaste of when, after Jesus was in death's grip, He was resurrected to life.

Jesus was telling the Pharisees that the greatest evidence that He is the Son of God would not be in the miracles, signs, and wonders He performed—it would be His resurrection from the dead after three days.

> *The Spirit of God, who raised Jesus from the dead, lives in you. And just as God raised Christ Jesus from the dead, he will give life to your mortal bodies by this same Spirit living within you* (Romans 8:11 NLT).

When the might of the Spirit raised Jesus, immediately the power of death and the grave was broken. The proof of this can be seen by the dead saints who rose and walked into Jerusalem to show themselves to people. Death is the ultimate effect of all sin—but Jesus overcame death and all the power of hell was broken. Hallelujah!

Then Jesus shouted out again, and he released his spirit. At that moment the curtain in the sanctuary of the Temple was torn in two, from top to bottom. The earth shook, rocks split apart, and tombs opened. The bodies of many godly men and women who had died were raised from the dead. They left the cemetery after Jesus' resurrection, went into the holy city of Jerusalem, and appeared to many people (Matthew 27:50-53 NLT).

Because Jesus conquered death, everyone who accepts His sacrifice can experience resurrection rather than death. Everyone who was resurrected before Him simply died because death still had power over humankind. Jesus' death on the cross and His resurrection three days later disarmed all of satan's authority and rendered his government's rule illegitimate: *"Having disarmed principalities and powers, He* [Jesus] *made a public spectacle of them, triumphing over them in it"* (Colossians 2:15 NIV).

The Resurrection of the Just and Unjust

I have hope in God, which they themselves also accept, that there will be a resurrection of the dead, both of the just and unjust (Acts 24:15 NKJV).

This verse in Acts 24 makes it clear that everyone will be resurrected. The thing that must be understood is that you will resurrect with the nature you died with. This is why Jesus being without sin is so critical to God's salvation plan for humanity.

The Bible makes it clear that not only will those who receive Christ and follow Him rise from the dead, but so will those who do not. When either group comes back to life by the power of God, they will then stand before Him and be judged. Those who do not receive the gospel of glory will be condemned. And Christians will be judged based on being conformed into Christ's image, the innermost parts of our hearts, and the specific calling that He called us to do for His Kingdom while we lived on earth.

> *At that time Michael, the archangel who stands guard over your nation, will arise. Then there will be a time of anguish greater than any since nations first came into existence. But at that time every one of your people whose name is written in the book will be rescued. Many of those whose bodies lie dead and buried will rise up, some to everlasting life and some to shame and everlasting disgrace* (Daniel 12:1-2 NLT).

Notice this passage of Scripture in Daniel 12 mentions that many of those who sleep will awake, some to everlasting life, and some to shame and everlasting contempt (NKJV). It's clear that when you rise, you are not necessarily perfected— you can still be unjust and also arise. Many believe that we wait until we die to become Christlike; however, I believe that we can be transformed into the image of Christ here and now as we behold His glorious Person through His word, and through supernatural encounters.

> *But we all, with unveiled face, beholding as in a mirror the glory of the Lord, are being transformed into the same image from glory to glory, just as by the Spirit of the Lord* (2 Corinthians 3:18 NKJV).

I believe that as we gain a revelation of Jesus Christ, a grace becomes available to be transformed from the inside out. Dying does not bring us out of sin. His powerful grace does. No matter what our struggles, the cross has made provision for our transformation. We can align with the reality of His precious blood and receive mercy through repentance. We can be changed forever—supernaturally upgraded.

> *Therefore, with minds that are alert and fully sober, set your hope on the grace to be brought to you when Jesus Christ is revealed at his coming. As obedient children, do not conform to the evil desires you had when you lived in ignorance. But just as he who called you is holy, so be holy in all you do; for it is written: "Be holy, because I am holy"* (1 Peter 1:13-16 NIV).

As you can see from this passage in First Peter, this brings us back to character. The grace of God is poured out in more abundance in areas where there is sin to give us divine power to overcome. No matter how powerful any demon is, you can be free right now in the greater power of God. Renounce sin; when you confess it to God sincerely, you receive the cleansing of the blood of Jesus.

The Glorified Body

There is another very important element of the resurrection I must share with you before we conclude this book. The resurrection of Jesus does not only bring us back to life after we "fall asleep." The resurrection restores our physical bodies to their original, immortal condition from before the fall.

This supernatural phenomenon will not take place until the return of Jesus. The sheer power of His return will cause such a dimension of glory in all the earth that people will meet Him in the air, and their physical bodies will be changed by resurrection power.

Every inch of the earth will be covered in resurrection glory. The apostle Paul told the church in Thessalonica—and tells us:

> *Brothers and sisters, we do not want you to be uninformed about those who sleep in death, so that you do not grieve like the rest of mankind, who have no hope. For we believe that Jesus died and rose again, and so we believe that God will bring with Jesus those who have fallen asleep in him. According to the Lord's word, we tell you that we who are still alive, who are left until the coming of the Lord, will certainly not precede those who have fallen asleep. For the Lord himself will come down from heaven, with a loud command, with the voice of the archangel and with the trumpet call of God, and the dead in Christ will rise first. After that, we who are still alive and are left will be caught up together with them in the clouds to meet the Lord in the air. And so we will be with the Lord forever* (1 Thessalonians 4:13-17 NIV).

This passage in First Thessalonians gives us the order in which the resurrection will take place. First Paul advises them that those who already have died will come with Him at His resurrection. They will be raised by the shout of an archangel and the sound of a trumpet. According to this verse, this will happen first. Then they will be caught up in the air. Last, those who are alive at the time of Christ's return will be caught up in the air with Him and those who were dead.

I want to pause and say that it's not important to fully understand how all of this unfolds. I just want to provide biblical insight. I want you to have a good grid of understanding for the glorified body. Another passage of Scripture that gives us detail into this is First Corinthians 15:

> *But in fact, Christ has been raised from the dead. He is the first of a great harvest of all who have died. So you see, just as death came into the world through a man, now the resurrection from the dead has begun through another man. Just as everyone dies because we all belong to Adam, everyone who belongs to Christ will be given new life. But there is an order to this resurrection: Christ was raised as the first of the harvest; then all who belong to Christ will be raised when he comes back. After that the end will come, when he will turn the Kingdom over to God the Father, having destroyed every ruler and authority and power. For Christ must reign until he humbles all his enemies beneath his feet* (1 Corinthians 15:20-25 NLT).

We are raised because Christ was raised from the dead. This is why the Bible says that Jesus is the firstfruit of them that slept (NKJV). At Christ's return, death's defeat will be enforced, leading to the mass resurrection of all who believed in the Messiah into His glory—death will be destroyed.

The doctrine of resurrections is not only about Christ's resurrection, but what becomes available through His victory over death and the grave. This leads us to our restored bodies. When we experience resurrection at His coming, our bodies will be changed. As our bodies encounter the glory of Jesus, the resurrection power will quicken our mortal bodies, which will become immortal and incorruptible. Much could be written on this topic; however, my focus here is to provide a general understanding of the overall doctrine of resurrections.

Again I turn to the apostle Paul for his Holy Spirit-inspired insight:

> So also is the resurrection of the dead. The body is sown in corruption, it is raised in incorruption. It is sown in dishonor, it is raised in glory. It is sown in weakness, it is raised in power. It is sown a natural body, it is raised a spiritual body. There is a natural body, and there is a spiritual body. And so it is written, "The first man Adam became a living being." The last Adam [Jesus] became a life-giving spirit.
>
> However, the spiritual is not first, but the natural, and afterward the spiritual. The first man was of the earth, made of dust; the second Man is the Lord from heaven. As was the man of dust, so also are those who are made of dust; and as is the heavenly Man, so also are those who are heavenly. And as we have borne the image of the man of dust, we shall also bear the image of the heavenly Man (1 Corinthians 15:42-49 NKJV).

In a moment, in the twinkling of an eye, at the last trumpet. For the trumpet will sound, and the dead will be raised incorruptible, and we shall be changed. For this corruptible must put on incorruption, and this mortal must put on immortality. So when this corruptible has put on incorruption, and this mortal has put on immortality, then shall be brought to pass the saying that is written: "Death is swallowed up in victory." "O Death, where is your sting? O Hades, where is your victory?" The sting of death is sin, and the strength of sin is the law. But thanks be to God, who gives us the victory through our Lord Jesus Christ (1 Corinthians 15:52-57 NKJV).

It's vitally important to understand that the glorified body, the divine nature of Christ in us through the blood, the awakening of our spirit to become a temple for the Holy Spirit, and the supernatural power of God are glimpses of our inheritance made available through the resurrection of the Messiah. Our inheritance would not be available without His resurrection. Everything we gained in this world and in the world to come is connected to the resurrection of our Savior, Jesus Christ. This is why speaking in other languages was not available until after the resurrection. The depths of divine language help us access our inheritance.

Blessed be the God and Father of our Lord Jesus Christ, who according to His abundant mercy has begotten us again to a living hope through the resurrection of Jesus Christ from the dead, to an inheritance incorruptible and undefiled and that does not fade away, reserved in heaven for you (1 Peter 1:3-4 NKJV).

The last but important portion of the resurrection doctrine is praying for those who have died to come back to life. This is extremely biblical and part of preaching the gospel of the Kingdom. Because Christ has authority over death, in His name we can command people who have died prematurely to come back to life. Every born-again believer can move in this supernatural feat.

My personal experience with resurrection took place three years ago. Though I have prayed for people who woke up from comas after drowning and people who were at death's door, the resurrection took place with my mother-in-law. Emily's mother had been sick for a very long time, and when the Lord called us to move to Florida from Columbus, Ohio, my wife and I followed the voice of God but it was a major sacrifice to leave my wife's mom. Thankfully, her siblings were there with her and we stayed in touch, but it was still a challenge.

After a few years, we received a phone call that Emily's mother had "coded out," was not breathing, and had no pulse. My wife's sister was in a panic so we began to pray. As we prayed, the power of God came upon my mother-in-law and she came back to life. We hadn't visited her for a while and although we felt it was actually her time to go, our good and faithful Father God brought her back to life so we, especially Emily, could see her mother one last time.

Her mother shared that she had left her body but heard our prayers and experienced herself returning to her body. We spent four days with her and Emily spent the night with her.

She graduated to be with the Lord as we were driving out of Columbus, Ohio, to return home.

Though this resurrection story did not lead to her living another twenty years, we believe it was her time. The Lord honored our desire to see her. It's important that we don't exaggerate the supernatural.

I believe that resurrections are going to become normal in this glory that is rising. As God is reviving His church, we will see the corporate body moving in revival glory. We will see resurrections of those who have just died, and resurrections of those who have been dead for many days. All glory to God!

Prayer

Father,

In Jesus' name, I thank You for the realms of Your glory. Cover me in the glory and bring me into Your glory. Today let me go from faith to faith, and glory to glory. I ask that You take me where I have never been before inside You. Manifest Your glory to me. In Jesus' name, amen.

CONCLUSION

Are you ready for the book of Acts to happen today? Do you want a move of God that is tangibly felt in this day and age like it was back then? That is what God desires us to long for. He is hoping we grab hold of the Acts of the Bible and put everything He has said, taught, and shown us into action. Acts back then should equal our actions here and now; and what was shown before should equal our current demonstration.

To move out into action, we must understand that the supernatural is not optional. With a mindset that has been supernaturally upgraded, we will know that the Good News that Jesus taught was confrontational. The gospel that the twelve disciples demonstrated is the very nature of God's Kingdom and His church. You can't demonstrate Jesus without moving in the supernatural. It is impossible to have one without the other.

Even now I believe that God is stirring divine hunger for the deeper things of God. There is a reason that in Psalm 42:7 (NKJV) David wrote, *"Deep calls unto deep."* There is a depth inside each of us that we have hardly tapped into because we are too surface-level focused to peer beyond the norm. Going in deep takes facing the unknown, which is not always easy—but I tell you it's necessary in these times. My friend, there is a well of untapped potential for the deeper things of God within you, and you must go after it.

It's time all believers delve beneath the surface. It's time we walk into greater dimensions of glory. There is so much more than where we are. We should be seeing *greater!* Jesus tells us:

> *Very truly I tell you, whoever believes in me will do the works I have been doing, and they will do even greater things than these, because I am going to the Father* (John 14:12 NIV).

Because Jesus says we *"will do even greater things,"* are we actually doing those greater works today? Let me answer that question for you. I believe we have misplaced the supernatural. Jesus is the supernatural. We can't have Him and then by default not step into the reality of the supernatural. They are one and the same…so get ready, because the time has come upon us for a supernatural upgrade!

About the Author

Chazdon Strickland is a loving husband to his beautiful wife, Emily, and father to four children. After an encounter with God, he was called to carry a global fire to the nations. Chazdon's ministry is marked with remarkable demonstrations of God's power, revelation of the Kingdom, apostolic signs and wonders, and fresh impartation to advance believers in the things of God.

IGNITE THE GLOBE stands as fresh fire of faith as one corporate body where the supernatural and apostolic fivefold graces are released. Our community is richly diverse, coming together to worship and serve. We welcome all people seeking God's love—our doors are open. The DNA of Ignite is Love, Integrity, Passion, Growth, Servanthood.

Chazdon and his wife are founders and leaders of Ignite Global Ministry in Jacksonville, Florida.

Contact Information
https://www.ignitejax.com/

Made in United States
Orlando, FL
14 March 2023

31031697R00109